Living with the Dragon

This book is intended as a supplementary text to any environmental ethics, business ethics, or business and society course and may also be used in a philosophy class studying unintended consequences. This book takes its title from J. R. Tolkien's admonition, "It does not do to leave a live dragon out of your calculations, if you live near him." The author argues that unintended consequences are a kind of live dragon that we should seek to minimize but that we unwisely have tended to ignore.

Ms. Daryl Koehn is the Cullen Chair of Business Ethics at the University of St. Thomas in Houston, Texas. She has a Ph.D. in ethics from the University of Chicago, an M.A. in politics, philosophy and economics from Oxford University and an M.B.A. in finance from Northwestern University. Her writings have been translated into many foreign languages, including Spanish, Chinese, Japanese, and Indonesian Bahasi.

Living with the Dragon

Thinking and Acting Ethically in a World of Unintended Consequences

Daryl Koehn

Routledge
Taylor & Francis Group

NEW YORK AND LONDON

First published 2010
by Routledge
270 Madison Avenue, New York, NY 10016

Simultaneously published in the UK
by Routledge
2 Park Square, Milton Park, Abingdon, Oxon OX14 4RN

Routledge is an imprint of the Taylor & Francis Group, an informa business

© 2010 Taylor & Francis

Typeset in Caslon by RefineCatch Limited, Bungay, Suffolk
Printed and bound in the United States of America on acid-free paper by
Edwards Brothers Inc.

Library of Congress Cataloging in Publication Data
Koehn, Daryl, 1955–
    Living with the dragon : acting ethically in a world of unintended
    consequences / Daryl Koehn.
        p. cm.
    1. Social ethics.   2. Consequentialism (Ethics)   I. Title.
    HM665.K64 2010
    170'.42–dc22   2009040705

ISBN 10: 0-415-87496-3 (hbk)
ISBN 10: 0-415-87497-1 (pbk)
ISBN 10: 0-203-85987-1 (ebk)

ISBN 13: 978-0-415-87496-0 (hbk)
ISBN 13: 978-0-415-87497-7 (pbk)
ISBN 13: 978-0-203-85987-2 (ebk)

For Julian and the Dragons of Isramadorn

Contents

Acknowledgements

I am grateful to my colleagues at the University of St. Thomas in Houston who participated in a short symposium series I moderated in the fall of 2008 on the subject of unintended consequences. Their objections and queries sharpened my thinking considerably. The probing questions posed by colleagues at various applied ethics conferences and symposia where I presented also helped clarify my thinking on this vexing subject.

Routledge publisher John Szilagyi's enthusiasm for the subject and project was a welcome spur to completing and polishing the manuscript. The professionalism of the entire Routledge staff throughout the production process was exemplary.

I would be remiss if I did not say a special thank you to

Thien Le, the assistant to the Center for Business Ethics at the Cameron School of Business at the University of St. Thomas. His help with the production and formatting of the manuscript was invaluable.

Hell is paved with good intentions.

Dr. Samuel Johnson

INTRODUCTION

In 1938, the economic sociologist Robert Merton lamented that, while many writers had touched upon the problem of unintended consequences, no one had offered a systematic treatment of them. Eighty years later, Merton's observation still holds true. Philosophers and theologians discuss chance and fate, but say almost nothing about the unintended consequences of human actions, policies, and laws. This oversight is understandable, given that most professors have little hands-on experience formulating and executing wide-reaching policies, devising products, or operating in markets. Uninvolved with actual consequences of choices, moralists and political theorists have largely neglected this vital subject. Theologians have dealt with unanticipated effects by attributing them to the unfathomable will of God and thus have avoided analyzing either the causes of these effects or the challenges they pose for moral evaluation and planning.

Economists and social scientists have been a bit more interested in the subject. They have tended, however, to focus on one specific area (e.g., the unintended consequences of welfare reform, of programs aiding battered spouses, of the deregulation of energy markets, etc.). Moreover, many social theorists have resisted considering untoward, unplanned outcomes. Desiring to model actions, they have treated humans as rationally self-interested beings who make optimal choices capable of being modeled by mathematics. Like theologians, this group of social theorists has been reluctant to admit the widespread existence of unintended and often non-optimal consequences, because to make such an admission would be to call into question whether sociology and economics are truly the sciences they claim to be.

Merton, his fellow social thinker Raymond Boudon, and the political theorist Jon Elster are exceptions.[1] These three academics have sought to provide a more general explanation of why unintended consequences of all sorts occur. Their works, though, do not include any discussion of the problems unintended consequences pose for moral evaluation in general. Nor do they provide much concrete guidance as to how we might avoid generating so many unfortunate effects.

This short book is intended to serve as a modest first step toward remedying these oversights. The first chapter develops a typology of unintended consequences and distinguishes them from historical contingencies. The second chapter analyzes some causes of unintended consequences, while the third explores the significant problems this class of effects poses for standard moral theories. The fourth and final chapter examines how we might begin to think and act so as to minimize unintended consequences. J. R. R. Tolkien is right to warn, "It does not do to leave a live dragon out of your calculations, if you live near him."[2] In Western lore, dragons may be benign or maleficent, but they are always powerful. In the East, the dragon represents the universe's infinite power to create that which is new and surprising. Unintended consequences are akin to a dragon, always present in the background of ever-changing daily life. The time has come for us to recognize just how pervasive these effects are and to begin routinely factoring them into our behavior.

1

PRELIMINARY DEFINITIONS AND DISTINCTIONS

What is an unintended consequence? An unintended consequence is an unenvisioned effect of a purposive act, law, or policy to which human beings and other organisms adapt their behavior. Although we certainly adapt to natural events—for example, after a hurricane we may decide to move out of a storm surge area—, social theorists reserve the category of "unintended consequences" for adaptive responses to purposive human action. This restricted usage makes sense, given that we typically are most interested in those consequences over which we have some degree of control. I will argue over the course of this book that unanticipated and unhappy adaptive responses to policies, rules and choices can indeed sometimes be foreseen and avoided.

The actions to which we adapt may be purposeful even if they do not appear completely rational. A woman may believe that eating two pieces of chocolate cake per day will keep her slim. She may be deluded in this belief, but her eating still qualifies as purposive or goal-oriented. She has chosen this strange diet with a view to achieving her desired end of staying slim. In what follows, I understand unintended consequences to result from actions traceable to a cause (choice, emotion, desire, policy, rule) that, in principle, lies within the control of a purposive agent. In other words, my focus will be on cases where those persons responsible for bringing about unintended consequences could have acted other than they did. The undesired outcomes I will be considering are not the result of some instinctual drive, biological tropism, or conditioned reflex outside the control of human agency.

It bears repeating that unintended consequences, as I understand the concept, are not foreseen. Consequently, I will not look at cases involving so-called "double effects." Double effects (which are widely discussed in the medical ethics literature) arise when an agent, in pursuing one desired consequence, brings about a second harmful and undesirable outcome. The doctor who administers morphine to allay the extreme suffering of a patient (the physician's intended and desired effect) may knowingly hasten the patient's death (a second undesirable effect). Some philosophers and clinicians defend this hastening as a morally excusable, unintended consequence of injecting morphine. I avoid this type of case because it is not clear that the second foreseen effect is unintended. Some thinkers contend that foreseen consequences never are truly unintended. After all, both the mitigation of suffering and the precipitating of death are foreseen and chosen by the doctor: The physician purposely opts to alleviate suffering because he thinks that this goal is worthy of being pursued, despite the known and likely side effect of hastening death.

The doctor consciously prefers to ease pain while hastening death over the option of doing nothing. Since examples of foreseen double effects do not involve adaptive responses, they are not especially relevant to policy-making and social theory. Nor do foreseen double effects pose the same challenge to moral theories as unwilled adaptive responses that, in some instances, are virtually unforeseeable by even the most prudent of agents. For these reasons, I will say nothing more about double effects.

Unintended consequences may be motivated by the best of intentions. Scientists devised a project to combat hunger in the Okavango delta. Beef cattle were substituted for native wild animals. At the same time, efforts were made to eliminate the tsetse fly that threatened cows. At first, the cattle thrived, and the people had plenty of meat. Over time, however, the burgeoning bovine herds overgrazed the land, leaving natives far worse off.[1] Their land, initially habitable, turned into desert, and the local people starved.

Development aid to Africa has helped reduce child starvation and doubled the number of children able to complete a primary school education in some countries.[2] The bad news is that much aid has been siphoned off into the private bank accounts of African leaders. Jeffrey Winters has estimated that the World Bank alone has been involved in corrupt loan fund deals worth about $100 billion.[3] There is another problem. Aid has undermined the role African governments should be assuming and has reduced citizens' ability to hold their leaders accountable:

A constant stream of "free" money is a perfect way to keep

an inefficient or simply bad government in power. As aid flows in, there is nothing more for the government to do—it doesn't need to raise taxes, and as long as it pays the army, it doesn't have to take account of its disgruntled citizens. No matter that its citizens are disenfranchised (as with no taxation, there can be no representation). All the government really needs to do is to court and cater to its foreign donors to stay in power. . . . Even what may appear as a benign intervention on the surface can have damning consequences. Say there is a mosquito-net maker in small-town Africa. Say he employs 10 people who together manufacture 500 nets a week. Typically, these 10 employees support upward of 15 relatives each. A Western government-inspired program generously supplies the affected region with 100,000 free mosquito nets. This promptly put the mosquito net manufacturer out of business, and now his 10 employees can no longer support their 150 dependents. In a couple of years, most of the donated nets will be torn and useless, but now there is no mosquito net maker to go to. They'll have to get more aid. And African governments once again get to abdicate their responsibilities.[4]

To take a domestic example of good intentions gone bad: When the US government moved to warn smokers of the dangers of tobacco, the tobacco companies responded by developing lower tar and nicotine cigarettes. These initiatives were initially well-received. Now it appears that the altered design of cigarettes has spawned a new form of cancer. Squamous cell carcinoma, which tend to appear in the larger air tubes of the lung, have given way to adenocarcinoma, which grow in the air sacs deep in the lungs. Researchers hypothesize that individuals who switched to filtered, lower-tar cigarettes have inhaled more deeply in order to get the nicotine hit to which they were accustomed.[5]

Unintended consequences may be positive or negative. The company Danone initiated its "1 Liter for 10 Liters" bottled water program to support the digging of new wells and retrofitting of old ones in dry areas of Africa. University students participating in the program felt that they were acting nobly and compassionately. If new wells were established, Africans would have fresh, clean water. While a few wells were dug, village elders in these towns soon discovered that it would not be wise to take advantage of all the assistance Danone was offering. Neighboring village leaders watched jealously as a few towns were chosen by UNICEF and Danone to get a well. Why, these envious elders wondered, weren't their villages chosen as beneficiaries? Leaders of the villages "lucky" enough to be chosen worried that, if they were to obtain several new wells, their neighbors might attack them in an effort to acquire water for themselves. If increased access to water were to lead to a sustained local war, the aided villagers would end up worse off than they were before they got the well. Not all the news is bad. The project did have one apparently desirable, unintended outcome. The wells funded by Danone meant that young girls no longer had to travel so far to get fresh water. Freed from the traditional female duty to carry water, these girls were able to enroll in the local schools and continue their education.

Unintended consequences, be they positive or negative, come about in a variety of ways. Frequently, people exploit some dimension of a situation or mechanism in a manner unforeseen by those responsible for initially creating that situation. Legislative loopholes are a classic case in point. Loopholes offer an opportunity for individuals to act in surprising ways not congruent with the spirit of the law. In the 1980s, when Congress defined a bank as an institution that both made loans *and* took deposits, it inadvertently opened the door for the proliferation of so-called "non-bank banks." These institutions only made loans *or* took deposits. Although there were regulations prohibiting interstate banking, many financial institutions were able to cross state lines by opening non-bank banks throughout the US. In this case, corporate managers availed themselves of a definitional loophole that legislators did not knowingly devise. In other cases, an action or policy establishes incentives for people to act in a way different from, or even opposite to, what the policy-maker or executive intends. Unintended consequences often appear when pay, risk, or cost structures are altered (more on this topic below). In still other cases, perverse effects emerge when human action (individual or collective) transforms the environment in such a way that people alter their lives in order to maintain their current standard of living or, in extreme cases, to survive.

In Chapter 2, I will sketch different types of causes of unintended consequences. But I confess upfront that I do not think it is possible to identify every possible cause. Human behavior is too complex and variable for us to be able to characterize every scenario. What one *can* say is that, in general, an unintended consequence results from complex interactions among (1) agents who freely act upon stated or unstated intentions; (2) parties who are affected by and react to those actions; and (3) other factors in the environment. A positive or negative unintended result may occur either instead of, or in addition to, a planned, willed consequence. The founding of non-bank banks was an unintended side effect accompanying the regulation of regular banks, the intended goal of the Bank Holding Company Act.

Historical Contingencies versus Unintended Consequences

An unintended consequence is not merely an untoward result of a trigger event. If that were the case, then every unfortunate historical contingency would qualify as an unintended consequence, and there would be little to analyze. The most we could say is that historical events do not follow immutable laws or, more poetically, "fortune governs events."[6] The unintended consequences that fascinate economists and sociologists—and that should interest philosophers and politicians—are not simply contingent effects or instances of good or bad luck. Rather, they are *unforeseen adaptations* to some alteration of the natural or social landscape brought about by purposive human action.

Just because an unanticipated effect of a choice or policy is unfortunate does not mean than an adaptive responsive has occurred. Consider the following two cases: When cities began to replace street side curbs with ramps to improve access for the disabled, no one thought the idea was bad or immoral. On the contrary, every moral system extols respect for persons. One way to show respect is to provide equal access to goods and services. Although a few critics carped about the projected expense of retrofitting streets, most citizens and urban planners believed it was morally right to enable those in wheelchairs or on crutches to move more easily about the city. After the fact, we learned that these ramps caused many serious accidents. Pedestrians found it difficult to remain upright when stepping onto icy sloped curbs.[7] Cities with curb cuts reported a marked increase in broken bones. The measure taken to aid the disabled wound up disabling more people.

A similar story has emerged with respect to truncated domes, the little bumps that the Americans with Disabilities Act (ADA) standards require on sidewalk ramps. According to John Wodatch, the Chief of Disability Rights Section at the Department of Justice,

> the idea behind the bumps or truncated domes was to give a physical clue to people who are blind that they were approaching a dangerous area, that they were approaching an intersection where there would be vehicular traffic. There was a lot of controversy about them because they were difficult to maintain. There were some groups of wheelchair users who maintained that they created a very uneven surface, which . . . for [those] in a fragile condition could be damaging to their health.[8]

Studies of truncated domes revealed that blind people found the bumps annoying and downright dangerous when wet. Meanwhile, city planners fretted over the prospect of lawsuits filed by women wearing heels who tripped on these little domes.

In these two cases, although the implementation of policies had untoward effects, people, by and large, did not change their behavior. Women still wore high heels, and citizens continued to step out onto curb cuts. These cases of broken bones are more akin to contingent events or instances of bad luck than to unintended consequences. Insofar as unexpected outcomes do not involve an unanticipated *adaptive response* to a rule, a course of action or policy, or to a change in incentives or cost structures, they are best understood as historical contingencies.

Let me be clear: I am not denying that historical contingencies may result in perceived harms or prove profound in their repercussions. George Herbert famously wrote:

> For want of a nail, a shoe was lost
> For want of a shoe, a horse was lost
> For want of a horse, a rider was lost
> For want of a rider, a message was lost
> For want of a message, a battle was lost
> For want of a battle, a kingdom was lost
> All for the want of a nail.[9]

The destruction of a kingdom is a serious matter. Yet the regime's downfall does not qualify as an unintended consequence of the lack of a nail but rather as an unhappy contingent effect. The poem sketches a chain of events. It does not portray human beings evaluating some purposive action of legislators, regulators, or executives, and then adopting a new course of action in response. Nor is there any question as to whether the loss of the rider or battle was, in principle, foreseeable. In the case of pure contingencies, we do not ask whether they were foreseeable. Yet the issue of foreseeability often *does* arise with respect to true unintended consequences.

The distinction between contingencies and unintended consequences becomes clearer and more plausible if one contrasts the unhappy contingent results of ADA-mandated truncated domes with the genuine unintended consequences the ADA had for employing disabled workers. Employers thought that the ADA would make it more expensive to hire disabled workers. Corporate managers were spooked by the prospect of having to alter facilities, provide specialized equipment, or redefine job responsibilities. Worried about lawsuits from protected disabled workers, employers post-ADA hired fewer men with disabilities. While most firms apparently did not shed current disabled workers already on the payroll, they did refrain from hiring any additional disabled workers.[10] Here we have a case where a significant number of business people consciously amended their hiring practices in response to what they perceived as a legislated increase in their cost structure. Their adaptive behavioral response qualifies as a true unintended consequence of the enactment of the ADA.

The response to the Endangered Species Act of 1973 (ESA) constitutes another adaptive change in behavior (i.e., it is a true unintended consequence). The ESA not only makes it illegal to kill animals belonging to an endangered species but also to damage the habitat of any protected animals that are on one's property. Under the ESA, the Federal Wildlife Services (FWS) essentially controls all wildlife, even if the protected animals are on private lands. Landowners who were deemed by the FWS to have endangered species on their land quickly discovered that their right to use the land had been transferred, in part, to the FWS and to those who have the agency's ear. Perceiving this alteration in their rights, owners responded by preemptively killing animals that might at some point be placed on the endangered species list. They went so far as to destroy native habitats so that endangered species would not come to live on their property. Data show that privately owned North Carolina forests were far more likely to be harvested if they were close to stands where red-cockaded woodpeckers, a protected species, live. It appears that landowners harvested these trees to avoid the possibility that the woodpeckers would move onto their land and thereby prevent the owners from being able to cut down trees. Discerning a threat to their rights, individuals altered their behavior (e.g., engaging in preemptive killings or habitat destruction) in order to preserve their freedoms.[11] Instead of protecting wildlife and habitats, the ESA legislation had the unintended effect of increasing the destruction of both in some cases. One begins to understand why Senator Hubert Humphrey was driven to quip, "The Senate is a place filled with goodwill and good intentions, and if the road to hell is paved with them, then the Senate is a pretty good detour."[12]

Types of Unintended Consequences

Unintended consequences, then, are not the same as contingencies. I will not say anymore about the latter. During the remainder of this chapter, I want to focus exclusively on unintended consequences, differentiating foreseeable from unforeseeable unintended consequences.

Foreseeable Unintended Consequences Involving Changes to Risk/Reward Ratios

Some unintended consequences, while not foreseen, are, in principle, foreseeable. In general, people do not assume greater risk without the prospect of greater reward. If we alter the amount of risk people are expected to bear, we should expect that they will demand higher compensation. Even before the passage of the Sarbanes–Oxley (SOX) law, prudent observers predicted that the law, by imposing more personal liability on board members, would make it more expensive for firms to recruit competent board members, especially directors to serve on audit committees. SOX would leave audit committee members vulnerable to lawsuits from disgruntled shareholders alleging that these directors should have known that the company was in severe trouble or cooking the books.[13] These governance specialists' prediction came true: Audit committee candidates adapted to the increased risk and responsibility by demanding greater compensation to serve on boards. This demand was a rational, foreseeable, and even predictable response to the change in the law. Legislators and regulators failed to anticipate this SOX effect, because they did not consider how directors would likely view liability under the new law. The consequence was unintended insofar as those responsible for drafting the law did not set out to make it more difficult and costly for corporations to recruit directors. Nevertheless, this outcome, I would argue, was foreseeable. History teaches us that individuals typically respond to heightened risk by requiring greater rewards.

There was another unintended but foreseeable effect of SOX. A few commentators forecast that not only new directors but also sitting board members would seek greater compensation after the law was passed.[14] Board members who get sued face uncomfortable questions from the press and must devote hours to being deposed. Although directors enjoy the income, networking, and power associated with board service, they are not eager to remain on a board if doing so may embroil them in a multi-year lawsuit and expose them to personal liability. Sitting directors calculated that SOX had made board service far riskier and, like new audit committee members, demanded to be compensated for the increased danger. We should not be surprised that director compensation increased across the board post-SOX.[15]

Foreseeable Unintended Consequences Involving Changes to Cost Structures

Policy making provides many examples of decisions that increase the costs of producers or consumers. These groups, in turn, alter their behavior in order to reduce costs, sometimes bringing about perverse results. These effects, while unforeseen by those regulators or policy-makers who increased costs, could have been anticipated. For we know very well that people generally try to minimize any costs imposed upon them.

In 2006, the state of Maryland passed a "millionaire tax" in an effort to balance its budget. The Annapolis lawmakers created a new upper income tax bracket. This law raised the top marginal income tax rate to 6.25%. Since other cities in Maryland (e.g., Baltimore) impose income taxes as well, the state–local tax rate soared to 9.45%. Although the *Baltimore Sun* predicted that the wealthy would "grin and bear it," the wealthy got the last laugh, relocating out of the state. Many of the wealthy own second homes in more tax-friendly locations, such as Florida and Virginia. It was easy for them to pack up and move. Instead of raising more revenue, Maryland tax receipts actually fell. Approximately 3,000 million-dollar tax returns were filed in 2008. That number dropped to 2,000 in 2009.[16] While some of the drop was likely due to the recession, the state comptroller has conceded that the decline was also caused by the rich moving out of the state. The Maryland government collects nothing on those missing returns. Instead of reaping a projected $106 million from the new bracket, the state lost money. Millionaires paid an estimated $100 million less in taxes in 2009 versus 2008—even at the new higher rates.[17]

The same flight of the rich from higher taxes has been documented in other states that upped the tax rate for upper brackets. High state income tax rates also appear to have had the unintended effect of slowing state growth rates and reducing wages.[18] In his 1998 study "Can State Taxes Redistribute Income?," economist Martin Feldstein concluded that not only will the rich move to avoid what they perceive as an unfavorable tax rate but also that "a relatively unfavorable tax will cause gross wages to adjust. . . . A more progressive tax thus induces firms to hire fewer high skilled employees and to hire more low skilled employees."[19] In other words, the average wage will fall in states with higher income tax rates. Feldstein's results are buttressed by Barry Poulson's recent study of why some states grew far richer than others from 1965 to 2004. Poulson found "a significant negative impact of higher marginal tax rates on state economic growth."[20] The increase in marginal tax rates on the wealthy produced the exact opposite of the legislators' stated goal of reducing the burden on the middle class.

The above examples illustrate a direct and immediate unintended but nonetheless foreseeable effect of imposing avoidable cost increases on taxpayers. Some unintended consequences are more indirect. Yet they, too, qualify as foreseeable insofar as the effects stem from changes to consumer or producer cost structures. Fuel economy legislation in the 1980s (Corporate Average Fuel Economy or CAFE) aimed at encouraging the production of less polluting cars. The legislation phased in different standards for cars and trucks with a view to favoring the manufacturing of more fuel efficient cars. Model year 1985 cars were to get 27.5 mpg, while trucks needed to average only 19.5 mpg. This legislated difference in standards has persisted for many years. Model year 2006 manufactured trucks had to meet an average of 21.6 mpg, while passenger cars faced a 27.5 mpg hurdle.[21] Seeing the looser standards for trucks, manufacturers avoided increased compliance costs by ramping up production of small trucks and sport utility vehicles. Consumers bought millions of these non-fuel efficient vehicles. As a result, mileage per gallon actually declined after the fuel-economy law was passed. In 1987, cars and trucks together averaged 26.2 mpg. By 2004, the average had fallen to 24.6 mpg.

CAFE had another unintended effect. Owners of more fuel-efficient vehicles tended to drive more miles because their gas bill was lower. More driven miles offset reductions in carbon dioxide emissions resulting from higher fuel efficiency. In addition, since the more efficient CAFE compliant cars were relatively more expensive than pre-CAFE cars, drivers had a financial reason to hold on to their cheaper gas-guzzling, high-polluting cars longer. If the CAFE standards had not been promulgated, those owners might have upgraded to used cars that did not meet CAFE standards but were more efficient than their old heaps. Whether these offsetting unintended effects (which were predicted by some economists) have been greater than the intended benefits of the CAFE standards (fewer carbon dioxide emissions, less reliance on foreign oil, less global warming) is hotly contested. What is *not* disputed is that the fuel economy standards, by affecting consumers' costs, have unwittingly caused many drivers to hold onto older, dirtier cars longer.

Foreign, as well as domestic laws, have increased costs, thereby generating perverse effects. In order to protect contract employees from exploitation, the Chinese government revised its labor law in 2007. The new law requires employers to hire contract workers as regular employees if they wish to continue to use these workers. The law permits contract workers to work for two fixed contractual periods (often five-year periods, but sometimes shorter). Workers may not be hired for a third such period unless the contract worker explicitly states that he or she prefers to continue as a fixed contract worker rather than become a full-time employee.[22] In the absence of such explicit consent, the worker must be offered an open-term employment contract. The new law further stipulates that employees who have already worked for a company for ten years or more without a contract must be offered an open-term (i.e., quasi-permanent) contract if the firm wishes to retain them. Open-ended contracts are considerably more expensive (up to 40% more costly) than fixed-term arrangements.

The Chinese government and its leaders did not adequately evaluate the possible effects of this new labor law, which created a clear incentive for employers to dump contract workers after two terms and to start anew with a fresh set of cheaper contract workers. A few pundits warned about this effect. The law was passed anyway. Although no formal studies have yet been done quantifying the effects of this law, many academics in China believe that the layoffs prompted by the new legislation have been substantial. *Forbes* reported that layoffs appeared to increase dramatically in response to the new law:

As trickles [of layoffs] turned into tidal waves, China's

media and analysts started to find a common denominator in these mass layoffs, pinpointing the high-risk groups: certain temporary workers, whom employers now must sign on at a greater cost, and staff that have served long tenures, who will soon receive almost ironclad terms of employment, all thanks to a new national labor law, effective January 1, 2008. . . . Huawei and LG Electronics, not coincidentally, targeted for job cuts those staff members who were approaching the ten-year limit.[23]

CCTV (the huge China telecommunications giant) and the Shenzhen school system fired many workers who were nearing the end of their second contractual term. China's central government has become so concerned that it has started pressuring companies behind the scenes not to lay-off workers. The law designed to protect employees has jeopardized them. Workers who would have been steadily employed on a renewable contract or no-contract basis now find themselves completely out of work.

The famous *Exxon Valdez* spill provides yet another example of a polar opposite, unintended consequence resulting from legislation that increased producer costs. After the 1989 disaster, many states along the East and West coasts passed laws assigning unlimited liability to tanker operators. One or two companies (e.g., Conoco) voluntarily adopted double hulled ships in order to reduce the risk of horrific spills. Other oil companies (e.g., Royal Dutch Shell) responded to this mandated increase in costs by outsourcing U.S. oil deliveries to independent shipping companies. These independent firms generally had little or no insurance and relied on older tankers that were more prone to leaking than the ships used by the larger, better established multi-national oil firms. While it is true that the number of large oil spills has steadily declined over the past fifty years, the fact is that huge spills were never that common and were already on the decline prior to the passage of the tanker laws. Most oil gets spilled in small accidents or in the form of steady leaks. The post-*Exxon Valdez* state laws inadvertently but foreseeably worsened the environmental situation by creating financial incentives for oil firms to outsource transport to older, leakier tankers.

Foreseeable Unintended Consequences Involving Changes to Compensation

Individuals do not like to see their standard of living decline. When laws or policies try to reduce the level of compensation, they produce unintended consequences that legislators and regulators ought to foresee and factor into their thinking. Just as we adapt to avoid increased costs, so, too, do we fight to preserve the income to which we have become accustomed and which we think we merit.

Although damage caps have been imposed in an effort to curtail the amount of medical malpractice damages awarded by juries, these caps have not been that effective. Lawyers paid on a contingency fee basis have continued to seek large damage awards. When caps were put on non-economic damage awards, plaintiffs' attorneys predictably shifted their focus from non-economic to economic damages, which often are not limited. The various components of damage awards are malleable, and so attorneys have been able to adapt. Despite the legislated caps, economic damages in medical malpractice suits have risen.[24]

In early 2009, the Obama administration proposed imposing a $500,000 annual compensation pay cap on executives in firms receiving bailout funds. The intent of the planned rules sounded good. The cap was meant to "insure that the compensation of top executives in the financial community is closely aligned not only with the interests of shareholders . . . but [also] with the taxpayers providing assistance to those companies."[25] Immediately upon hearing of this proposal, compensation specialists and corporate lawyers predicted that such caps would prove ineffective, if not downright dangerous. Companies might respond by changing the titles of executives; reassigning managers to subsidiaries not following within the scope of the law; re-pricing stock options to make them more valuable; or granting restricted shares or stock options not subject to the cap.[26] Or certain functions in the firm might be outsourced, with companies spinning off trading or underwriting operations. In that case, what firms did with taxpayer money might become harder to monitor and control.

The proposed pay cap rules were worrisome in a second way. They prohibited executives from cashing in any preferred stock until the firm had paid the taxpayers back. When the payback was complete, though, executives could cash in all of their preferred stock. Some politicians speculated that the payback provision would have the perverse effect of increasing risk to taxpayers if managers assumed greater risks in the hope of getting their preferred stock payoff sooner.[27]

Not all foreseeable unintended consequences derive from legislation. The private sector has produced its share of compensation-related perversities. In the 1980s, Harvard's Michael Jensen and other finance professors urged firms to compensate board members using stock options. The professors maintained that the board's interests would be more closely aligned with those of the firm if the directors prospered only when the firm did. Alignment was supposed to encourage board members to discharge their fiduciary duties of care and loyalty to the firm in a more mindful way. Dozens of firms rushed to adopt stock option plans for directors. As it turned out, finance professors and corporate governance experts were overly optimistic about directors' integrity. They forgot that board members might be tempted to overlook wrongdoing by management when a significant proportion of their own paychecks was suddenly linked to the firm's financial performance.[28] When board members of a company hold hundreds of thousands of dollars worth of that company's stock, they are in danger of losing independence and failing to discharge their duties. If directors come to believe that corporate management is corrupt, they have a duty to disclose possible wrongdoing to regulatory authorities and law officials. However, going public with these problems usually lessens the value of board members' holdings. Directors who are paid cash retainers pocket the cash regardless of how the company does; by contrast, directors paid with stock options are left holding virtually worthless pieces of paper if the stock depreciates. Options-paid directors have a substantial incentive to turn a blind eye to fraud in order to preserve their options-based income stream. As some philosophers predicted, many directors altered their behavior in line with this huge financial incentive. In this case, the market's attempt to achieve better director performance through alignment arguably produced the exact opposite effect. It worsened director performance by creating incentives that severely compromised board member independence.

I have been discussing untoward adaptive responses that could have been predicted (and, in some cases, were warned against in advance by outside commentators). Past adaptations to increases in costs or risk or to decreases in compensation offer some guidance as to what is likely to occur in the future if we alter such things. In other cases, though, the unintended consequences may be unforeseeable even by the most prudent of agents. Sometimes the past is of little help to us. What sorts of effects fall into this category?

Unforeseeable Unintended Consequences That Are Especially Brazen or Ingenious

Unintended outcomes are less foreseeable when people respond to laws or pressures by behaving in an especially brazen or criminal way, going so far as to risk the death penalty. During the past two decades, multi-national companies (MNCs) switched production capacity to China and other parts of Asia in order to reduce labor costs. The historical record shows that many critics worried that foreign sweatshop owners might exploit workers. But few, if any, commentators anticipated that Asian manufacturers, in response to relentless pressure from importers to lower prices, would risk murder charges by incorporating poisonous materials in goods exported to the U.S. and Europe. Nor did scholars or business people foresee that MNCs would find it almost impossible to control the quality of materials used by clever Asian suppliers desperate to continue production at any cost. Mattel (despite having a highly touted quality control process) was forced to initiate three recalls of toys contaminated with lead paint. The firm's September 2007 recall involved toys coated with lead paint as late as August 2007, weeks after Mattel had begun to crack down on suppliers and initiated other lead-related recalls.[29] In retrospect, we can see that outsourcing was a product quality disaster in the making. In the future, we can think about possible perverse responses by suppliers. At the time when the outsourcing began, however, the possibility of manufacturers *knowingly* producing deadly products was not seriously entertained by anyone.

Wildly creative adaptive responses are another class of difficult to foresee effects. Seeking to preserve its rural, pastoral views, the state of Vermont banned roadside billboards and huge signs. Ever ingenious, small businesses adapted by erecting huge sculptures on their premises.[30] Today Vermont is home to a carpet store capped by a massive genie and an auto dealership with a twelve foot gorilla grasping a full size Volkswagen Beetle. The state's legislators and environmental groups did not intend to promote wacky signage. I could not find any commentator who anticipated that the anti-billboard law would result in Vermont's roads sporting behemoth horses and squirrels wearing red suspenders. Proponents of the law were completely taken aback by this inventive adaptation by businesses.

Some actions lead to both foreseeable and unforeseeable unintended consequences. When companies began to pay managers with stock options, some governance experts objected that managers might diddle the earnings to drive up the stock price in order to make their options more valuable. They were right to be concerned. Earnings were fudged.[31] What critics did *not* foretell was that managers would shamelessly backdate stock options in order to increase their compensation by insuring that their stock options had value regardless of whether the firm itself performed well or badly. Manipulating earnings was foreseen. Widespread managerial backdating of options was not expected, because no one thought that managers and directors would be so bold as, in essence, to print money for themselves.

Unforeseeable Unintended Consequences Far Afield from the Original Intent

Sometimes an unintended consequence is so removed from the agents' initial intentions that the effect in question will be virtually impossible to predict. Back in the 1980s, the federal government created the Resolution Trust Corporation (RTC) to dispose of the assets of failed savings and loans companies (S&Ls). The RTC hired some clever people who figured out how to securitize and sell the assets of these S&Ls. Regulators and legislators did not antici-pate that people throughout the financial markets would change their thinking and begin to view *all* assets as things to be converted into sellable securities. Their innovations spawned the mortgage-backed securities, which lay at the heart of the subprime mortgage crisis. The solution to one crisis quite unexpectedly laid the foundation for another debacle thirty years later. In this case, the unintended con-sequence of our solution to the S&L crisis is probably best characterized as unforeseeable, given that the subsequent massive transformation in how market makers thought about the world of finance was distant in time and different in nature from the regulators' much narrower intent to save the S&Ls.

To take a non-market example of an adaptation dis-tant from the original intent: Mosquito nets donated by developed countries to Zambia with a view to stopping the spread of malaria have been sewn together by villagers to make fishing nets. As a result, fish stocks have been dramatically depleted as hungry fishermen have removed fish, eggs, and spawn from rivers. This over-fishing almost certainly will lead to widespread hunger in the future. Yet no one considered this effect of the well-intentioned dona-tion on the food chain because the two issues of malaria and over-fishing seem, on the surface, so disparate.

Unforeseeable Unintended Consequences That Are Subtle Perverse By-Products of Choices

The final category of possibly unforeseeable consequences involves subtle by-product effects that take years to emerge. Over a decade ago, large institutional investors sought to minimize risk by switching to index funds. Prior to that switch, major investors (who picked particular stocks and took sizeable positions in these companies) had a powerful incentive to monitor these firms' activities and to work closely with CEOs. Once these institutional investors started placing money in index funds, they inevitably spread their equity holdings much more thinly. Investing in the market as a whole, they no longer had any interest in monitoring every single company whose stock they had purchased. They adapted by withdrawing from intense engagement with CEOs and boards of directors and curtailed their monitoring of individual firms. The large investors' index fund strategy worked handsomely for many years. Only during the recent tsunami of corporate financial frauds and restatements did institutional investors realize that their risk-reduction strategy had actually left them more vulnerable to fraud-related losses. Index funds appeared so obviously to reduce risk in a direct way that large investors did not register the subtle indirect way in which their reduced scrutiny of firms increased the odds that they would lose money.

The preceding typology of unintended consequences is not exhaustive, but it is, I hope, sufficiently comprehensive to give some feel for the lay of the land pertaining to these effects. What, though, causes the various types of unintended consequences? And how should we evaluate and address them? These questions require chapters of their own.

2
CAUSES OF UNINTENDED CONSEQUENCES

What are the causes of unintended consequences? Conservative political commentators attribute them to overly zealous legislators and policy-makers who act upon what they take to be good intentions and ignore possibly adverse side effects. These politicos' attitude is supposedly one of "other consequences be damned." The reality, though, is far more complex. The causes of unintended consequences lie in the nature of the world, in practical freedom, and in the operations and habits of the human psyche.

Worldly Causes

Complexity and Rapid Change

As Adam Smith recognized centuries ago, the world's complexity is a major cause of unintended consequences, some beneficial, others malign. In particular, Smith thought that we cannot know in advance exactly how people will assess their interests and modify their behavior. Since people calculate their self-interest in different ways, and since the effects of various actions may cancel each other out, we "can only know afterwards, and not beforehand, whether the summation of their actions leads to emergent order or disorder."[1]

The unpredictability of this inherently complex world of interests and actions is not the only issue. Rapid change creates difficulties for choice as well. Organizations increasingly employ what management theorist Peter Drucker has called "knowledge workers." These are employees who own the means of production—their intelligence. Knowledge workers are expected to anticipate developments and devise creative responses to the changes they foresee. But because human beings are incredibly adaptive; and because, as Smith noticed, changes interact in a myriad of ways, each inventive response devised by these same knowledge workers risks bringing about difficult to foresee and hard to control unintended consequences. We are always behind the proverbial eight ball.

Ricardo Hausman of Harvard's Center for International Development offers a nice example of the challenge posed by knowledge workers' innovations: "Ten years ago, no one thought about regulating credit default swaps because credit default swaps didn't exist. . . . What's endemic to financial crises is that the rate at which we innovate is greater than the rate at which we learn from them."[2] Knowledge workers are bound to act in ways that precipitate unanticipated adaptations simply because they are working with quickly evolving situations and factors well outside their comfort zones.

Unintended consequences are a large part of the modern employee's steep learning curve and should be accepted, a point acknowledged by some companies.

> There is a story that Thomas Watson, the founder of IBM, once asked to see a newly promoted vice president who failed on his first assignment and cost the company a million dollars. The young man reported to the IBM chief, ready for the worst. "I guess you called me in to fire me," he said on entering Watson's office. "Fire you!" said Watson. "We just spent one million dollars as part of your education."[3]

Watson's attitude, alas, is rare. Most firms continue to blame knowledge workers for unintended consequences that occur simply because these employees' past actions (and those of other players in the system) bring about dramatic transformations in the marketplace and in the world at large that frequently are too complex, swift, and dynamic for any one person to comprehend fully.

Master of the Universe Mentality

To cope with increasing complexity, we rely ever more on technology. Such reliance, which the modern world's scientific mindset encourages, generates unintended consequences. The German philosopher Hans Jonas has documented how the world is more and more shaped by modern science, while at the same time this development of science has alienated us from nature. Today we see nature as something that exists in order to be manipulated by man. We have unconsciously adopted the view of the early modern scientist Francis Bacon: "The sovereignty of man lieth hidden in knowledge. . . . Now we govern nature in opinions, but we are thrall unto her in necessity: But if we would be led by her invention, we would command her by action."[4] This "Master of the Universe" mentality has led us to put our faith in technology and to think that we can predict and master things and systems beyond our ken and control. Our technology chases and then bites its own tail. This dynamic is readily apparent in the world of software development. The latest software programs offer new functionality. At the same time, they contain flaws or features exploited by hackers who proceed to limit, destroy, or hijack that very functionality. These hackers modify their approach as fast as new security systems and controls come onto the market.

According to Jonas, the stakes involved in human action are higher than they have ever been. Our hubristic mentality has put the very existence of the human race at risk. The development of nuclear weapons, the adoption of lifestyles that increase carbon dioxide and warm the earth, the contamination of air and water—all of these threaten our ability to find good food, breathe clean air, and bear and rear healthy children. Jonas locates the root of our drive to dominate nature through technology in the ancient teachings of Gnosticism, a view that true man is a spirit trapped in a physical body. Gnosticism portrays men and women as uniquely different and separate from other animals. Existing apart, we feel driven to make our own destiny, dominating our environment.

Jonas seeks to counter that Gnostic impulse by

emphasizing our kinship with all of living nature. Contending that all organic life is inherently purposeful, he urges us to rethink our supposedly unique human condition. Human beings have a goal or purpose to be realized not in some alternative spectral, Gnostic spiritual world (where we have escaped from our physical bodies) but right here in the physical world we share with the other animals. What is that purpose shared by all organisms? To be free. It "is in the dark stirrings of primeval organic substance that a principle of freedom shines forth for the first time within the vast necessity of the physical universe—a principle foreign to suns, planets, and atoms."[5] Whereas "matter remains self-identical, life is self-mediating and self-transformative. Life's formal independence versus inorganic nature manifests itself in the internal identity of the organism above and beyond all metabolic transformations it might undergo."[6]

Jonas' emphasis, on the one hand, on our organic nature and, on the other hand, on our metabolic ability to maintain our integrity through changes in the environment points both to a cause of unintended consequences and to a possible remedy for them. Insofar as we are organic beings, we are irremediably dependent on nature. We are part and parcel of it and, therefore, should not think of ourselves as its masters. Such hubris seduces us into making massive technological interventions (e.g., Three Gorges Dam; Mississippi River levees) that redound upon us in harmful ways. The interdependent world is such that every attempt to dominate nature risks enslaving us further. As long as we think of ourselves as purely spiritual, masterful beings, we will thoughtlessly blunder about creating unintended consequences:

> [S]o formidable and potent have the new technologies at humanity's disposal become that they *have rendered obsolete 2,500 years of ethical discourse.* Heretofore, humankind's interventions in the natural world were limited in scope, and their consequences were readily foreseeable. For this reason, the balance between humanity and nature was never fundamentally in doubt. No such assurances can be provided concerning the impact of modern technology, which, contrary to all precedents, has already permanently altered the earth's biosphere in numerous respects and which continues to do so in ways in whose consequences have yet to be fully determined. . . . Traditional approaches to ethics— Aristotle's "phronesis," Kant's "categorical imperative"— were accustomed to dealing with human action that fell within well-defined and familiar parameters. . . . Under the radically changed situation inaugurated by technological modernity, however, ethical prescriptions that are merely oriented toward "the good" (Aristotle), or that rest content to treat persons as "ends in themselves" (Kant), might well prove defenseless in the face of the worst case scenario of ecological catastrophe (italics mine).[7]

Our mental models are not nearly as complex as the environment in which we live. When our mental models and hypotheses do not mirror the world's complexity, a dangerous "human gap" develops.[8]

Jonas' second theme—our metabolic ability to preserve ourselves through change—provides a basis both for concern and for hope. The ability to change ourselves is precisely what gives rise to unintended consequences (understood as organic beings' adaptive responses to alterations in rules, policies, laws, etc.). Sometimes our adaptations seem worse than that to which we are responding. But there is good news as well. Our adaptive power gives us a measure of autonomy, permitting us to learn from past actions and to adjust our behavior with a view to minimizing unintended consequences as we go forward. We can change the way we think and act if we adopt a new more ecological outlook, a possibility I explore in the concluding chapter.

A Newtonian Mindset

A second equally prevalent mindset has contributed to the proliferation of unintended consequences. The biologist Robert Ulanowicz has shown how Western thinking about systems has long been in thrall to a Newtonian worldview. This worldview has five distinctive features, each of which has kept us from being able to better anticipate and think about unintended consequences.[9]

Newtonian systems are characterized by determinism. Scientists assume that, in principle, we can calculate the subsequent position of every particle or thing in a system if we know its initial position, the forces operating upon it, and the stable closure conditions. Each position is assumed to be calculable and predictable. Organic social systems and ecosystems, though, are not deterministic. We rarely, if ever, know exactly how to characterize the initial conditions—e.g., what exactly was the beginning point or initial condition of the financial crisis we are now experiencing? Knowing the initial conditions would not be that useful anyway, because determinism does not hold at the micro-level where quantum physics rules.

We may be able to identify certain propensities that will affect how events unfold. Propensities, however, are not identical with unchanging, universal laws. As we saw in Chapter 1, sometimes unintended consequences exhibit features that render them more foreseeable (e.g., they are rooted in changes to risk/reward ratios or to cost structures). It does not follow, though, that we will ever be able to identify all such features. Even if we could do so, we still would not have a completely determined system, because the various types of consequences—be they intended or unintended, foreseeable or unforeseeable—could well interact in surprising ways.

This last point brings me to the second feature of Newtonian systems—they are closed. The only forces assumed to operate within the system are those identified within Newton's theory. Mysterious forces have been identified that do not fit nicely into a Newtonian worldview. Physicists have shown the existence of spooky action at a distance. Two entangled objects are mutually dependent such that when one object is altered, the other instantaneously changes even when it is a vast distance away from the first object. How and why such an instantaneous response occurs mystifies scientists. Organic developments or successions rarely unfold in the same way. Chance plays a significant role in developments, as do the ignorance and choices of extremely adaptable agents within the system. These factors are not considered within closed systems: "Chance is ... the Achilles heel of Newtonianism. ... For, if there are (as Newton assumed) only material and mechanical causes at work, a chance event that cannot be subsumed by the law of averages would disrupt the reductionists' scenario."[10] I am not claiming that all unintended consequences are the result of chance. Rather I am suggesting that we will not be able to improve our grasp of such consequences as long as we think of the human world as a closed system. Factors continually operate and interact in surprising ways, and our approach to analyzing the goodness of proposed actions needs to be rethought to take that fact into account.

Newtonian systems are not only deterministic and closed. They are also treated as reversible. Time's arrow points both ways in physical systems. Social, economic, and ecological developments, by contrast, are not reversible. These enter the realm of unalterable history. Once General Motors has gone bankrupt, no one can reverse the process and restore GM exactly to its pre-bankrupt state. After a species has become extinct, we cannot go back in time and resurrect it. As long as we implicitly adhere to a Newtonian worldview, we will not appreciate just how high the stakes are for us. As Jonas foresaw, the risks associated with human actions have increased exponentially. Self-inflicted human extinction is now a real possibility. Fully acknowledging the historicity of our deeds is a necessary first step toward better preparing ourselves to cope with foreseeable and unforeseeable unintended consequences.

Atomism is a fourth characteristic of Newtonian thinking. The notion of reversibility presupposes that wholes can be broken down into stable, smallest units or entities and then rebuilt from these least units. Human social and economic systems are not decomposable in this way. Organic systems function as wholes that are more than the sum of their parts. Comprehending that whole requires us to observe the parts in interaction with each other. We cannot resolve to least units and then treat these atoms in isolation from all other parts. Some processes do not operate at lower or partial levels. As Adam Smith surmised, behavior of parts in isolation can differ spectacularly from what we see when these parts are evaluated within the larger whole. Unintended consequences arise because human beings modify their behavior in response to changes in other parts of the social, economic, and natural system. Neither agents nor the altered parts exist in isolation. It would be more accurate to think of this system as a giant spider web. Even a minute change in one part of the web vibrates throughout the entire whole.

Universality is the fifth Newtonian dimension that must be rethought. Newton assumes that the system is governed by unalterable universal laws. These laws always arise as part of an observation of a specific part at a particular point in time. Yet this

idea that a law . . . formulated within a particular window of time and space should be applicable all the time and everywhere seems limited to [those] circumstances where systems parts are rarified and interact weakly. . . . Ecology

teaches its practitioners somewhat more humility. . . . While
the organic approach [will encompass some rules and laws],
organic principles seem to pertain to limited ranges of space
and time.[11]

We are not living in a world of weak interactions but in a
net of strong adaptations. Our principles correspondingly
need to be more modest. They should be taken less as
universal laws and more as rules of thumb.

All of these five characteristics of the modern Newtonian
mindset ought to be, if not jettisoned, reconceived in a
more humble, ecological, systems thinking-based manner,
a point I will return to in Chapter 4.

Cultural Diversity

While Smith, Drucker, Jonas, and Ulanowicz locate the
cause of unintended consequences in modern developments, complexities, and inadequate or dangerous worldviews, one ancient thinker believed the cause lay in how
human beings respond to the diverse nature of humanity.
Long before modern scholars began to think about
unintended consequences, the Greek historian Herodotus
investigated the cause of the war between the Persians and
Greeks. Collecting and reflecting on a wealth of anecdotes
involving nations' customs, practices, and chronicles, he
explored how disparate peoples interpreted each other's
deeds and speech. Herodotus arrived at a dramatic conclu-
sion: We think we understand far more about our foreign
friends and enemies than we, in fact, do. Seduced by this

illusion of omniscience, we involve ourselves in trans-actions (e.g., wars) destined to go awry, because both sides have fundamentally different self-understandings. Project-ing our individual and national self-understandings onto others, we unwittingly and systematically misinterpret what we see and hear and then adapt to the false image we have created of others' motivations.

Consider the tale with which Herodotus begins his account of the cause of the war between the Greeks and the Persians.

The Persian chroniclers say the Phoenicians caused the feud. The Phoenicians came (the Persians say) from the so-called Red Sea to our sea, and having settled where they still live today, they immediately started voyaging great distances. . . . They came to other lands, including Argos. At that time, Argos was pre-eminent in what we now call Hellas. Arriving then at Argos, they displayed their wares. Five or six days after they came, . . . many women went down to the shore, including the king's daughter, whose name was, the Greeks and Persians agree, Io, the daughter of Inachus. While the women were making their desired purchases, . . . the Phoe-nicians yelled to each other and swooped down on the women. Most, they say, got away, but Io and some others were carried off . . . to Egypt.

This is the Persian, though not the Greek version, of how Io came to Egypt and of how the injustices began. After that incident, the Persians maintain, that certain Greeks (whose name they can't tell) stopped at the Phoenician city of Tyre and seized Europa, the king's daughter. . . . At this point, the wrongdoings were, according to the Persians, balanced until the Greeks committed a second misdeed by sailing in a long ship to Aea in Colchis and the river Phasis . . . and carrying off Medea, the daughter of that country's king. When the Colchian king sent a messenger to Greece demanding reparations for the loss of his daughter and demanding that she be restored, the Greeks (the Persians say) retorted that, because the Persians had not made reparations after abducting Io, they, for their part, wouldn't make any to the Colchians.

The story goes on to say, that in the next generations, Alexander, Priam's son, having heard this tale, thought he would obtain a Greek wife for himself by means of rape and robbery, for he was convinced that he would not have to make any restitution because the Greeks hadn't done so. So he seized Helen. At first, the Greeks determined they should send messengers to demand her return and seek satisfaction as well for their loss. But when they made this proposal, the Trojans brought up the rape of Medea, and reminded the Greeks that they had not made reparations in that case nor given up Medea. So did they now expect satisfaction from others?

Up until this juncture there was only plunder on both groups' part. But henceforth (the Persians insist) the Greeks bore the greatest share of blame. For they invaded Asia before the Persians went into Europe. "We think it unjust of men to kidnap women, but to avenge such seizures is foolish, for the wise ignore such matters as the women clearly would not have been carried off if they hadn't been willing participants. We took no account of the rape of women carried off from Asia; the Greeks, however, gathered a huge force, came to Asia, and destroyed Priam's power. After this, we have always viewed the Greeks as our enemies." The Persians claim Asia and all the barbarians who dwell therein as theirs; Europe and the Greek peoples they take to be entirely separate.

This is what the Persians say about the matter; and in their view, the capture of Troy marks the beginning of their quarrel with the Greeks. For the Persians claim, as their own, Asia and all the barbarian people.[12]

This beginning of Herodotus' *History* is remarkable in several respects. Note how the Persians claim Priam, the king of Troy, as an Asian, while the Greeks understand the Trojan war more as a battle between Greeks—the leaders on both sides speak Greek and share a love of martial honor and courage. The Persian claim is geographical: The whole Asian region is theirs, regardless of the ethnicity of those who happen to live in Troy or elsewhere. The Greeks, by contrast, conceive of Greek-ness not in geographical terms but in moral/political/ethnic terms.

Moreover, the Persians have confused a *story* involving the rape and abduction of the mythical creatures Io and Europa with a *factual account*. The Persians as a matter of fact invaded Greece, attacking the Athenians and Spartans. Io and Europa, by contrast, are fictional or archetypal women who appear in differing myths told by Greeks, Egyptians, Phoenicians, Persians, Lydians, etc. Having mistaken Homer's tale of Achilles' rage and Apollodorus' story of the voyage of the Argonauts for factual histories, the Persians append these faux histories to the myth of Io and Europa to create their own supposedly true chronicle. Without realizing they are doing so, the Persians seamlessly conflate what the Greeks would distinguish as fiction versus fact.

The Persians interpret the beginning of the conflict in purely personal terms: A dispute over women was the cause of the war. As Herodotus stresses, it is the Persians who say that the conflict was a case of tit for tat. Although the Persians reduce the political to the personal, Herodotus himself locates the cause of the war in an act of aggression by a flesh and blood historical leader: "I will single out that man whom I myself know started unjust acts against the Greeks. . . ." That man is Croesus, the Lydian king who was "the first of the barbarians that we know conquered some of the Greeks and forced them to pay tribute, while making friends of others."[13] For Herodotus, the war between the Greeks and Persians is about a people's freedom and its right to be self-determining: "Before Croesus' rule, all Greeks were free."[14] Herodotus is going to exercise his very Greek freedom to think for himself, relying not upon stories told by the Persians (or, for that matter, by Greeks or anyone else) but upon what he personally has been able to discover about the factual cause of a political act of aggression by one people against another. The title of his work—*History*—literally means in Greek "investigation."

Don't get me wrong: Herodotus is certainly not averse to stories. He repeatedly tells us what other peoples say about themselves. For these tales reveal how the Persians, Egyptians, Greeks, and other nations understand themselves and their neighbors. As Herodotus later shows, it is the Persians, not the Greeks, who are wont to start fights over women. Although the Persian chroniclers' condescendingly pronounce that the avenging of rape is a matter only for fools, the stories told by the Persians themselves portray their satraps repeatedly as engaging in precisely such revenge. Herodotus' opening account of how the Persians describe the cause of the war can thus be read as an example of the human psyche's shadow side at work as the Persians attribute their misdeeds to the Greeks. The Persian version of the cause of the conflict with the Greeks itself functions as a factor in the war insofar as the Persians have unknowingly projected their unacknowledged personal–political worldview onto their victims. Successive Persian rulers' belief that they understand their Hellenic foes leads them to underestimate this enemy. For their part, Greeks are not sufficiently aware that the Persians do not think of political freedom in terms of a shared language and the right to self-determination.

The two peoples' inability to understand each other results in their talking past one another. Each side reacts in ways that produce massive unintended consequences. In their mutual non-comprehension, Greeks and Persians are paradoxically alike. Indeed, all of us unconsciously mix fact, fiction, and projection. Then we act upon our constructed illusions. It is no wonder that Herodotus is driven to remark that cities that "previously were great . . . have now become small, and those that in my time were great were at an earlier time small . . . so well I know that man's happiness never remains in the same place. . . ."[15]

Organizational Diversity

Not only cultural but also organizational diversity spawns unintended consequences. Organizational behavior theorists McKinley and Scherer have identified tensions that develop between the managerial and executive group/class and lower level employees during corporate reorganizations.[16] The executives who are planning and executing the changes feel empowered and in control. They experience a "reassuring sense of cognitive order."[17] Meanwhile, the subordinates who fear being re-assigned, demoted, or fired are experiencing cognitive disorder. They may respond by resisting change. At this point, a second tension comes to the fore. While the executives are confidently proceeding to implement change in accordance with their vision, the environment is, in the short term, becoming ever more chaotic. In order to reassert order, the executives opt to implement more changes. That strategy, in turn, has the unintended consequence of initiating a vicious cycle of change, making the working milieu ever more disordered.

Guowei Jian makes a similar point, detailing the very different interpretive schemes used by management and subordinates.[18] Management may meet with consultants and financially interested parties and decide upon a plan of change, such as the introduction of Total Quality Management (TQM). Executives then publish new organizational charts and start to implement the change in light of the understanding of TQM they have evolved through contact with outsiders. Lower level employees view this initiative through a lens shaped by routines and by their firm-specific past experiences with changes and with particular managers. Their lens reflects what they have come to value in their workplace—e.g., the fact that their firm has been family friendly. Employee "interpretations of change emerge when employees reconstitute meaning of [managerial action and pronouncements] within their own interpretive schemes. *Interpretive tensions between employees and senior management set up conditions for unintended consequences to emerge*" (italics mine).[19]

Practical Causes

I have been considering the possibility that the complexity and the inter-relatedness of the world, the diversity of its peoples and classes, and our inherited worldviews are responsible for unintended consequences. There is, however, another class of cause. The philosophers Hannah Arendt and Ludwig von Mises locate the cause of unintended consequences not in these factors but in the nature of action itself.

Arendt uses "action" as a technical term for an activity distinct from both labor and work. Labor refers to the ceaseless repetitive activity needed to sustain life. Working in a rice field year after year qualifies as labor. Work differs from labor insofar as work yields a lasting artifact, and the production of this artifact is a process with a beginning and end. The carpenter who makes a set of kitchen cabinets has done work in creating a product that will endure for years to come. Action is, Arendt believes, a higher form of activity than labor or work. Action alone allows our humanity to show forth. In acting, we reveal to the world what we are—beings who are free to bring new practices, institutions, conditions, and children into the world. Action is not unqualifiedly good. We do not (and cannot) control how our deeds and personalities are construed by others. Nor can we reverse what we have done. Still, action is free in a way that labor and work never will be. Labor binds us to the earth and biological necessity; working is governed and controlled by the requirements of the end product. Only action approximates a purely free activity.

Although action brings the possibility of fame and glory, its very freedom challenges our desire to control and regulate daily existence. The difficulty is not simply that the unpredictability of action requires that we practice forgiveness (a practice which Arendt heartily endorses). The larger problem is that we are operating without a moral safety net and without firm criteria to use when making choices. We literally do not know what we are doing. Nevertheless, we proceed as though we possess certain knowledge of outcomes, relying upon an improper understanding of judgment. We wrongly construe judgment as the act of subsuming the particular under a universal law or category. Since human action creates the world anew, there are, Arendt contends, no unchanging, pre-existent universals under which to subsume the particular case at hand. Unintended consequences will always occur as free choice brings novelty into the world. Other people's responses to our deeds equally make the world anew. Perhaps by reconceiving practical judgment, we may be better able, in the absence of control, at least to comprehend the effects of action and adjust our behavior accordingly. If we proceed with our current false notion of judgment, we risk inadvertently making matters worse. Outdated irrelevant universals prevent us from grasping the meaning and significance of what we are doing in the here and now. Lacking a correct understanding, we reactively adapt our behavior in unhelpful ways.

Mises, too, stresses the connection between uncertainty and action. Unintended consequences testify to the essential freedom of all human action:

> The uncertainty of the future is already implied in the very notion of action. That man acts and that the future is uncertain . . . are only two different modes of establishing one thing. . . . [T]he fact remains that to acting man the future is hidden. If man knew the future, he would not have to choose and would not act. He would be like an automaton, reacting to stimuli without any will of his own. . . . Natural science does not render the future predictable. It makes it possible to foretell the results to be obtained by definite actions. But it leaves unpredictable two spheres: that of insufficiently known natural phenomena and that of human acts of choice. Our ignorance with regard to these two spheres taints all human actions with uncertainty. . . . Every action refers to an unknown future. It is in this sense always a risky speculation.[20]

Despite our deliberate efforts to control our fate, "there is in the course of human events no stability and consequently no safety."[21] Some dimensions of human behavior may be captured by economic laws describing discernible patterns of behavior (e.g., when prices of a good go up, demand for that good usually falls), yet every specific action manifests unique features not graspable by economic analysis or scientific laws. Individual and highly particular acts generate unintended consequences, and—Mises contends—always will do so. Mises and Arendt agree on the fundamental point: Action and its effects are inherently unpredictable. Human practical freedom is itself a major cause of unintended consequences.

Psychological Causes

The operation and habits of the human mind are a third type of cause of unintended consequences.

Mistaken Assimilation of Present to Past

Success breeds failure as our past triumphs tempt us to trust too much in systems, strategies, and policies that have worked in the past. The novelist E.M. Forster describes this phenomenon as mental atheriosclerosis:

> Unfortunately there comes to the majority of those of middle age an inelasticity not of physical muscle and sinew alone but of mental fiber. Experience has its dangers: It may bring wisdom, but it may also bring stiffness and cause hardened deposits in the mind, and its resulting inelasticity is crippling.[22]

Merton echoes Forster in attributing this lack of flexibility and paucity of imagination to acquired habits:

Error may intrude itself . . . in any phase of purposive action: We may err in our appraisal of the present situation, in our inference from this to the future objective situation, in our selection of a course of action, or finally in the execution of the action chosen. A common fallacy is frequently involved in the too ready assumption that actions that have in the past led to the desired outcome will continue to do so. This assumption is often fixed in the mechanism of habit and it there finds pragmatic justification, for habitual action does in fact often, even usually, meet with success. But precisely because habit is a mode of activity that has previously led to the attainment of certain ends, it tends to become automatic and undeliberative through continued repetition so that the actor fails to recognize that procedures which have been successful *in certain circumstances* need not be so *under any and all conditions.* Just as rigidities in social organization often balk and block the satisfaction of new wants, so rigidities in individual behavior may block the satisfaction of old wants in a changing environment (italics in original).[23]

In the modern era, this crippling mindset frequently takes the form of a naive and habitual overdependence on technology. Technological advances have helped us in the past, so we expect them to do so in the future. This confidence is frequently misplaced. To take just one example: The Titanic's crew and passengers knew that their ship had been designed and built using the latest technology, and so they trusted too much in its safety system. The result was as disastrous as it was unexpected.

Our sclerotic approach to existence leads to unwanted

effects by preventing us from discerning that which is unprecedented in our situation. Conditioned by our habits to assimilate the novel to the familiar, we may not immediately realize that, in fact, we are dealing with a brand new phenomenon. As Arendt has noted, European Jews initially (and catastrophically) assumed that the Third Reich was engaged in another pogrom of the sort Jews had suffered many times in the past. The hateful instigators of pogroms would kill some Jews; then the murders would cease. The Jews had no inkling that the Nazis were planning the systematic extermination of every Jew in Europe. By responding in traditional ways to what appeared to be a pogrom, the Jews unintentionally fell victim to a genocide motivated not merely by hate but by Nazi ideology. Of course, even if the Jews had right away grasped the peril they were in, they likely still would have been victimized. Arendt does not deny the Jews' vulnerability but wants us to focus on how our failure to recognize how human action remakes the world leads all of us to respond in habitual ways that inadvertently compound the dangers of our situation.

Biological Impulsiveness

Sometimes unintended consequences that might have been foreseen are overlooked because we get so caught up in the present moment that we cease to try to assess future risks objectively. Recent work by economists has documented the crucial role played by what John Maynard Keynes called "animal spirits." Animal spirits refer to non-economic motives and irrational behaviors that motivate choice.[24] Economists and social scientists have been rediscovering what the ancients knew and what some modern biologists have long suspected: "Although many of us may think of ourselves as *thinking creatures that feel*, biologically we are *feeling creatures that think*" (italics original).[25] Or as the Enlightenment philosopher Jean-Jacques Rousseau put it, "The human understanding owes much to the passions." Indeed, our understanding develops because we are creatures of passion: "We seek to know only because we desire to enjoy, and it is not possible to conceive why he who has neither desire nor fear would go to the trouble of reasoning."[26]

Our brain attaches feelings to what we sense as these perceived impressions are processed through our limbic system. We can learn to use our higher brain functioning to generate concepts and stories capable of suppressing or altering these feelings. So I am not saying that we are enslaved by emotions. Reason has its own interests. It remains true, though, that many of our behaviors are motivated by feelings of pain and pleasure and by a desire to avoid the former and to experience the latter. We find costs painful and rewards pleasurable, which is why, as we saw in Chapter 1, changes in cost and incentive structures can have outcomes diametrically opposed to what well-meaning policy makers and pundits envisioned.

When we have a success, we unconsciously feel that we will inevitably prosper if we repeat what worked in the past. This felt belief gives rise to over-confidence—what the behavioral economist Robert Shiller has dubbed "irrational exuberance." Over-confidence causes the economy to expand too quickly, causing financial or real estate bubbles. Conversely, when we experience a disappointment, we unwarrantedly project that experience into the future and infer our situation is more dire than it actually is. Such undue pessimism may unintentionally prolong recessions. If people, out of fear, save too much money, then they can bring about the very economic depression their government is desperately trying to avoid. In such cases, our limbic system, not our cerebral cortex, is governing our lives and engendering dangerous misperceptions and maladaptations.

Hormones can significantly distort judgment. University of Cambridge researchers monitored bodily changes occurring in securities traders as they made investment decisions. These researchers documented what endocrinologists label "the winner's effect." Looking at men and women who risked up to $2 billion as they sought to trade and capitalize on small price changes in stocks, the investigators found that individuals who began the day with relatively high levels of testosterone made more money over the course of the day. Each additional success raised the level of testosterone, boosting confidence and leading to more profitable trades. Those traders who had learned to harness such hormonal changes were more successful than those who simply responded uncritically to the testosterone boost. The best traders seemed to be aware that too much testosterone might impede their ability to evaluate risks accurately and cause them to take on too much risk.

These same researchers found that traders' levels of

cortisol, which the body releases in response to stress, varied wildly, sometimes increasing five-fold. Cortisol depressed confidence, making the traders more fearful. This fear limited their ability to think clearly.[27] As with the observed testosterone effects, the unintended consequences developed not as agents responded to other people's actions and choices but as they reacted to their own past successes and failures. In this case, biology set up a vicious circle. Losing increased cortisol levels, which made individuals reactive and more fearful, leading to still more losses.

> Dr. John Coates, lead author [of the study], said, "Rising levels of testosterone and cortisol prepare traders for taking risk. However, if testosterone reaches physiological limits, as it might during a market bubble, it can turn risk-taking into a form of addiction, while extreme cortisol during a crash can make traders shun risk altogether." Coates, himself a former trader, continued, "In the present credit crisis, traders may feel the noxious effects of chronic cortisol exposure and end up in a psychological state known as 'learned helplessness.' If this happens central banks may lower interest rates only to find that traders still refuse to buy risky assets. At times like these economics has to consider the physiology of investors, not just their rationality."[28]

The only way out of this physiological cycle is for us to monitor our reactions carefully, becoming aware of the symptoms of hormonal flux. If our hormonal surges can be taken in hand, then we can better identify and mitigate undesirable consequences that may result from our deeds.

Stubborn Adherence to Plans

Some writers have downplayed the problem of unanticipated risks. They talk as if once we discover that elusive Theory of Everything all will be well in the world. Charles Handy has pointed out how delusional such talk is:

> The more turbulent the times, the more complex the world, the more paradoxes there are. We can, and should reduce the starkness of some of the contradictions, minimize the inconsistencies, understand the puzzles in the paradoxes, *but we cannot make them disappear, or solve them completely, or escape from them.* Paradoxes are like the weather, something to be lived with, not solved. . . . (italics mine).[29]

Uncomfortable with paradox, uncertainty, and ambiguity, we devise plans aimed at solving thorny problems once and for all. Problem-solving in itself is not a bad thing. We human beings live by our wits. The harm begins when we make a plan and conclude that we have definitely hit upon the right approach. Systems theorist Dietrich Dörner's research into why our projects so often fail spectacularly is relevant here. Dörner found that subjects would adhere to their initial plan even after they started getting indications that their strategy and tactics were seriously flawed. It seems that we crave simplicity and do not want to face having to revisit our original choice and refine it in light of additional data.

No doubt the mental sclerosis and habits that worried Merton and Mises are partly to blame for our stubborn adherence to our first plan. Having drawn upon our experience with what worked in the past to draft that plan, we prefer to stick with a proven winner. Wishful thinking plays a role as well. Research has revealed that we consistently focus on data supporting the outcome we desire and ignore information supporting other possibilities.[30] This psychological fixity prevents us from anticipating and heading off unintended consequences. Perceptual fixity accompanies psychological fixity. In one famous experiment, participants were asked to select the more attractive of two faces appearing on their computer screen. As they started to move the cursor toward their choice, the experimenters flashed a bright light on the screen. At that moment, the computer system switched the pictures. Most subjects post-flash moved the cursor in the original direction and so chose the "wrong" picture. Not only did they not notice the switch until they were told of it, they denied that they had erred, providing elaborate post-hoc justifications for their mistaken choice.[31]

The fact that some subjects reassessed what they were seeing after the flash shows that we can learn, as the yoga masters recommend, to live in the present. Psychology is not destiny, but liberating ourselves from perceptual-psychological fixity clearly is not easy.

Poor or Teleopathic Framing of Issues

Our tendency to frame issues poorly reflects and feeds this dual perceptual–psychological fixity. The debate over whether America should have a nationalized health care system assumes that there are only two delivery systems: a single payer (e.g., national government) or multi-payer (e.g., private insurance companies collect premiums and pay the bills). This framing excludes other possibilities. A hybrid system might be possible. Or we could allow states to experiment with a view to discovering which system works best in, say, Hawaii or Texas. The overly narrow framing of options prevents us from imaginatively entertaining other possibilities. If we instead collectively explored the pros and cons of a variety of proposals, we would have a chance to hear others speculate about how people might alter their behavior under different health care scenarios. Their voiced insights could then be used to improve our options. We lose this opportunity for refinement when we unwittingly blinker ourselves through restrictive framing.[32]

Poor framing typically derives from teleopathy, the sickness of focusing too much on a single goal. In this case, the problem is not so much acquired habits or an emotional limbic system response but rather an intense focus on a single goal. I suspect that evolution has favored this constriction of our field of vision. Predators able to concentrate on a particular animal are more likely to kill their prey. What we forget is the downside of this intense focus. Perceptual experiments show that, when we are intent on achieving a goal, we filter out any information that might distract us from attaining it. In another famous experiment, subjects were asked to watch a video of young people on either a white or black team. Each team tossed a ball among its players. Viewers were told to count the number of tosses completed by members of the white team. Midway through the video a man in an ape suit walked among and through the ball tossers. The vast majority of viewers did not see the interloper. Only when they were told to watch the video a second time without focusing on the counting task did they register the man dressed as an ape.[33] The subjects in this and other similar experiments were looking but they were not seeing. Consequently, they failed to "use or share highly relevant, easily accessible, and readily perceivable information during the decision-making process."[34]

It is easy to see how teleopathic blindness contributes to unintended consequences. Long before the recent spate of perceptual experiments by psychologists, Merton sounded the alarm about what he called "the imperious immediacy of interest."[35] He was convinced that legislators frequently so desired a particular outcome that they became blind with respect to other possible effects of their acts. In many of the policy related and legislative examples given in Chapter 1, representatives who were too invested in a position did indeed bring about the exact opposite of what they hoped to accomplish. What the latest experiments and biological findings show is that teleopathy is not confined to our leaders. Each of us is prone to acting upon desires so controlling that we do not stop to consider adaptive responses that, in principle, might be foreseeable. Instead, we plow full steam ahead.

Unbridled Rush to Exploit Opportunities

It should be stressed that ill-considered laws and regulations are but one manifestation of teleopathy. Sometimes *the lack of regulation* operates as a contributing cause, especially in the case of new markets rife with opportunity for those cunning enough to spot chances to profit. In the absence of regulation, it seems that every financial instrument created to serve some specific, legitimate purpose quickly evolves into a speculative tool as traders adapt their behavior to exploit the new instrument. Unintended consequences occur because we are self-interested beings who seem to be hard-wired to scan for opportunities to benefit ourselves.

Darwinians would see survival value in such behavior: When resources are in scarce supply, those who can act quickly are more likely to secure life's necessities. However, a single-minded rush to exploit opportunities can prove pernicious as well. Consider the unintended effects of credit default swaps (CDS).

Credit Default Swaps (CDS) were originally designed for owners of debt instruments (corporate bonds, asset-backed securities, mortgage-backed securities and loans) to purchase insurance against the possibility of default. By purchasing default insurance the catastrophic risk was transferred from the owner to the risk underwriter. . . . This practice of default risk underwriting debt still exists, and serves the purpose of allowing risk to be transferred from one party to the next. However, in recent years the use of Credit Default Swaps has expanded well beyond the notion of risk transfer. . . . The CDS market is unregulated. It allows any "player"— underwriter (seller) or buyer—to participate in this market. Anyone can participate in a swap, betting on the likelihood of a debt instrument defaulting, or credit spreads widening or narrowing, without the necessity of owning the underlying instrument ("reference debt"). To place these bets, no cash, or little cash, is required. . . . With $60-plus trillion in swaps outstanding, it is fair to assume that a large number of sellers (underwriters) are not financially able to make the necessary payment when required. . . . In effect, the CDS market has morphed into a highly speculative, unregulated arena where fortunes are made and can be quickly lost—quite the opposite of its original intent, which was to create a vehicle for mitigating risk. This perversion has substantially increased the risk for the vast majority of major financial players to the point of potential catastrophe.[36]

A similar analysis could be applied to Special Investment Vehicles (SIVs) and other financial instruments, all of which elicited perverse adaptive responses from creative and cunning traders and investment bankers who discerned in these unregulated instruments a way to make a fast buck. Having contributed to the demise of the financial system, many of these whiz kids now unexpectedly find themselves without a job and with poor prospects of future employment.

Modern High Anxiety

The final psychological cause I wish to discuss is the most difficult to describe. Many Westerners suffer from what the French philosophers Alexis de Tocqueville, Jean-Jacques Rousseau, and Montesquieu characterized as an inquietude of the spirit. By "inquietude," they meant "the state of a man who is not at ease, the lack of ease and tranquility of the soul, which is in this regard purely passive."[37] Montesquieu and his French counterparts traced this unease or anxiety to the loss of religion. Our infinite longing for the transcendent, no longer able to fulfill itself in union with God, has metamorphosed into an infinite love of self. In our vainglory, we have begun to worship ourselves.

What justifies this transformation of lowly human base metal into divine gold? What makes us worthy of such great love? If our lives had intrinsic worth, then perhaps this self-worship might have some basis. Do they have such worth? Over time Christianity inadvertently undermined the classical Greek and Roman position that differing ways of life—the life of pursuing money, fame, virtue, and wisdom—possess varying degrees of intrinsic satisfaction and worth. Christianity glorified only one life—the life of believing in and serving God. As creatures in the image of God, human beings shared in divine worth. When Christian belief began to wither away, that source of dignity disappeared as well. Bereft of classical insights, people no longer had any idea of whether a commercial, artistic, or contemplative life would prove more satisfying.

In fact, modern thinkers such as John Locke ridiculed the classical idea that some ways of life were intrinsically better than others:

> Hence it was, I think, that the philosophers of old did in vain
> inquire, whether *summum bonum* (the chief good) consisted
> in riches, or bodily delights, or virtue, or contemplation: and

they might have as reasonably disputed, whether the best relish were to be found in apples, plums, or nuts, and have divided themselves into sects upon it. For, as pleasant tastes depend not on the things themselves, but on their agreeableness to this or that particular palate, wherein there is great variety; so the greatest happiness consists in the having those things which produce the greatest pleasure, and in the absence of those which cause any disturbance, any pain. Now these, to different men, are very different things. . . . [T]hough all men's desires tend to happiness, yet they are not moved by the same object. Men may choose different things, and yet all choose right; supposing them only like a company of poor insects; whereof some are bees, delighted with flowers and their sweetness; others beetles, delighted with other kinds of viands, which having enjoyed for a season, they would cease to be, and exist no more for ever.[38]

In other words, all lives are equally good and satisfying insofar as people pursue what they relish or find attractive. Something is not desirable because it is good; it is good because we happen to desire it.

This change in the understanding of the good life has had two major consequences. First, it has stimulated citizens of democracies to seek to distinguish themselves at almost any cost; and second, it has fueled materialism. Let us begin with the first effect. Insofar as work or activities no longer possess any intrinsic satisfaction for us (remember activity is good because we desire it, not the reverse!), we understandably have begun to doubt whether our life is good. In order to convince ourselves that we are, in fact, living well and worthy of respect, we seek to elevate themselves above the common masses. Tocqueville was struck by how the more equal a country becomes, the more people desperately strive to distinguish themselves. The quest for fame and what we today know as celebrity was anticipated by Montesquieu who postulated that the average person was motivated by a sense of anxious uneasiness. Political liberty by itself does not guarantee citizens psychic tranquility. Quite the reverse. The doomed attempt to appear superior to our fellow human beings fuels a restlessness of mind and spirit. People are forever plotting how to get ahead. This desperate plotting underlies the tendency to rush to exploit opportunities discussed above. Upon visiting America, the French nobleman Alexis de Tocqueville was struck by the "avidity" with which

> the American hurls himself on the immense prey that fortune offers him. . . . He braves without fear the arrow of the Indian and the maladies of the wilderness; the silence of the forests offers him no surprises; the approach of savage beasts moves him not: A passion stronger than the love of life unceasingly spurs him on. Before him there extends a continent almost without limits, and one would say that, fearing that he has already lost his place within it; he hastens in fear of arriving too late.[39]

This insight brings us to the second consequence of the loss of intrinsic worth. People have sought to regain their place in the universe by doing outrageous things to get noticed. A cursory glance at YouTube videos and blog postings suffices to verify this point. When we are not performing attention-getting stunts, we are running after the latest greatest electronic gadget or newest handbag. By owning that which no one else yet possesses, we seek to fool ourselves into thinking that we are special. Materialism emerges hand in glove with the restless elevation of the self.

Driven hither and thither by irrational and somewhat desperate inquietude, we unwittingly create all sorts of unintended consequences. Some of these fall into the foreseeable category. Students who put pornographic videos of themselves on the Internet do not intend to make themselves unemployable. Yet these students should not be surprised to discover that potential employers surf the Internet and google for information about job candidates. After all, the whole reason for electronically transmitting provocative pictures and screeds is to garner public attention. The young forget that, if their peers can view their postings on blogs and social networking sites, strangers can do so as well.

In other cases, the Internet's liberation of human initiative and avidity has been wondrous indeed. Not even the strongest booster of computers anticipated that, by 2009, twenty typical California households would create as much digital trafficking as the entire Internet did in 1995.[40] What is especially surprising is how users have taken the computer—originally conceived as an information processor—and morphed it into an engine propelling us out of the information age into the recommendation age.[41] Power is shifting from experts and talking heads to ordinary consumers and smaller players. At present, the majority of consumers (62%) look at online peer reviews; they research products online (69%) and use computers to do price-comparison shopping (39%) and to ferret out coupon codes.[42] Use of search engines, such as TripAdvisor and Shopping.com, have democratized searching and put downward pressure on pricing. Democratic and material-istic cultures want ever more stuff at ever lower prices. Consumer pull is replacing producer push techniques. Consumers are not only making recommendations to their fellow purchasers but providing the products as well. The "hit-driven" economy is giving way to a proliferation of niche products with consumers making and posting videos and blogs and bypassing stores, middlemen, and other established players to sell their art and other creations on sites such as ebay, Etsy, and Craigslist.

Many more causes could be added to the categories of worldly, practical, and psychological causes. My aim in this chapter has not been to categorize every such cause but rather to say enough to persuade the reader that unintended consequences are not rare or arcane happenings, and to show that coping with them will require working on many fronts. We need to take them seriously, especially because they pose a deep and systematic challenge to standard moral philosophizing about action and choice. To that issue I now turn.

3

THE CHALLENGES UNINTENDED CONSEQUENCES POSE FOR STANDARD MORAL FRAMEWORKS

By now it should be clear that human actions often, as Aristotle likes to say, "miss the mark." When unintended consequences are far afield from the original goal or when adaptations are especially brazen or creative, no one—not even the most prudent person—may be able to discern the true meaning and significance of an action, choice, law, or policy. Time lags contribute to the difficulty. Months or years may have to elapse before the unhappy effects become apparent.

Nor do we get any respite. Unintended consequences never cease arising. Whenever we exercise our practical freedom, we bring newness into the world. Assimilating the new to the old, we fail to appreciate that we are, in fact, facing an unprecedented challenge. The goodness of that which is truly novel is hard enough to assess under the best of conditions. Evaluation is made still more difficult by our arrogant Master of the Universe and universalizing Newtonian mindsets and by our prejudices, biases, and teleopathies. In light of all of these challenges, how should we set about evaluating whether a proposed act is good or not? How should we render judgment and make choices? Standard moral theories do not offer especially satisfying answers to these questions.

Utilitarian Morality

Utilitarianism maintains that an agent's action, policy, or rule is morally good if and only if it produces the greatest net utility or happiness (or the smallest net loss of happiness) for the largest number of people when compared with alternative actions, rules, or policies the agent might endorse.[1] The theory asks us to do a net cost–benefit analysis for every proposed course of action. Since it is impossible to calculate the effects of proposed alternatives with respect to every single person in the world, utilitarians typically focus on classes of relevant people whose utility is likely to be affected in some significant way by the proposed action. Unintended consequences pose difficulties for even this more restrictive approach.

The agent must first identify alternative courses of action and then perform a cost–benefit analysis comparing each course's benefits and costs to classes of affected parties. This comparison presupposes that agents are able to specify in advance the most salient consequences of each of the actions to be assessed. If a particular sort of unintended consequence has occurred regularly in the past and so qualifies as possibly *foreseeable*; and if we assume that these utility evaluators possess finely-honed foresight, then those doing the cost–benefit analysis may be able to factor in some unintended consequences when performing this moral calculus. In Chapter 1, we saw that a change to an incentive or cost structure often yields perverse consequences. In principle, utilitarians could assign a negative value in a case involving such an alteration. However, even when adaptive effects may be foreseeable, utilitarian evaluators still may overlook other effects, which their prejudices, biases, perceptual fixities, or teleopathic desires prevent them from seeing. Libertarians, for example, are adept at seeing the downside to government interventions but typically ignore possible benefits. Liberals, conversely, perceive benefits of government programs but tend to overlook the possibility that beneficiaries will adapt to these programs in perverse ways.

Utilitarianism offers no account or mechanism by which agents become more prudent over time and better able to cope with unintended consequences. Doing cost–benefit calculations will not in and of itself refine people's ability to render sound judgments. If an evaluator is already biased toward one outcome, then doing the calculations risks degenerating into a self-validating exercise that merely confirms the bias. In that case, even foreseeable unintended consequences may slip through the utilitarian net of calculations. In those more problematic cases where proposed courses of action generate *unforeseeable*, unintended consequences, utilitarian calculations will not have much value. Course A may initially look to be morally preferential to course B on utilitarian grounds. After the fact, A may look far less good than B because of the unintended consequences resulting from the choice of A. Of course, if course B had been preferred to A, a similar reversal of perspective might have occurred, because B might also have had unforeseeable unintended consequences. In general, utilitarianism is too mechanical to deal with the hugely creative and dynamically adaptive responses of free human beings. In a world with major unforeseeable, unintended consequences, flipping a coin may produce just as morally good outcomes as utilitarian calculations.

Deontological Morality

A deontological morality, such as the one articulated by Immanuel Kant, stipulates that a course of action is morally good (or at least morally permissible) if and only if the maxim of the action does not involve the agent in a practical contradiction. The agent must be able to will the maxim or practical description of the envisioned action in a consistent way. Only actions that do not involve us in a contradiction and that thus accord with our rational nature have genuine moral worth and truly respect human nature.[2] In Kant's language, only when we act on non-contradictory maxims do we treat people as ends in themselves, rather than as means.

It is not, according to Kant, morally permissible for an agent to say, "I will make it my maxim to commit suicide because I will be better off if I kill myself than if I go on living." In this formulation, the would-be suicide inconsistently projects the self into the future, imagining herself as continuing to live and reaping benefits even after she has killed herself. Post-suicide, there is no "I" who could be better off dead than alive. As Kant puts it, the suicide's maxim is not consistent with a system of nature organized around the idea of self-preservation through self-love. When we analyze the maxim, we see at once that "[this system of nature] . . . would contradict itself and would therefore not subsist as nature" understood as a system of self-love.[3] Since the suicide's maxim cannot be consistently willed, Kant deems her action morally wrong. By contrast, if a manager of a firm proposes, "I will make it my maxim to pay the firm's employees the highest wage I possibly can while providing appropriate returns to all other stakeholders," there is no obvious contradiction in the maxim itself and so this action would qualify as morally permissible on deontological grounds.

The difficulty with the deontological approach is that formulating the maxim correctly requires insight into the meaning of the proposed action. Unless the agent possesses a highly refined sense of the many possible consequences of the action, his maxim of the action will not capture the action's true practical significance. Suppose we consider whether it is morally permissible to introduce some organism into an environment to counter a threat to human life posed by another organism. We hope and intend that the introduced counter-pest will prey upon and eliminate the threatening life form. If human life is, as Kant insists, "beyond price," sacrificing some apparently threatening predators (or even an entire animal species) appears to involve no contradiction. It seems that we can consistently say, "I make it my maxim to introduce counter-pests in the environment to remove another pest posing a serious threat to human life." The plan seems to qualify as a morally permissible course of action.

But will the artificially induced change to the environment, in fact, preserve human life in the long run? The counter-pest may ultimately pose a much greater threat to human beings than the organism we initially feared. Introducing new predators or prey into an ecosystem almost always causes organisms to adapt their behavior in response to new opportunities or threats. We may discover in hindsight that, instead of using the neutral-sounding term "counter-pest," we should have formulated our maxim to read, "I will make it my maxim to introduce another potentially human-threatening organism into the environment in order to remove a serious threat to human life." In that form, a contradiction starts to emerge, and the action becomes morally questionable. The problem is that we discover the correct terminology or phrasing of the maxim only *after* we have acted in accordance with our seemingly good initial maxim and perhaps inadvertently destroyed much of the human race. It is of dubious moral value that any remaining survivors will be able to tell themselves, "Well, at least our maxim seemed to be consistent at the time we willed the action, even though the effects of the action showed our maxim was actually radically inconsistent."

Unless we have honed our ability to discern possible consequences of proposed actions, we will neither be able to formulate our maxims well nor be able validly to assess their consistency. To the extent that unintended consequences are frequent, widespread, perverse, and sometimes completely unforeseeable, it is doubtful whether any one person has the requisite individual foresight needed to anticipate these effects and to build them into his or her maxims. Even if we were to grant that more prudent individuals are better able than their rash peers to formulate maxims capturing the full import of proposed actions, that concession will not save deontological reasoning. Two problems remain. First, deontologists do not base their morality on prudence. Instead, they claim, as Kant does, that being moral is within the reach of everyone whose basic reason is intact. Supposedly any rational being can correctly formulate and then adequately assess maxims.[4] Second, even the most far-sighted person in the world will not anticipate *all* unintended consequences *every* time. There will always be cases where an action initially deemed to be straightforwardly morally permissible on deontological grounds will appear, after the effects emerge, to be either outright immoral or at least possibly so. Deontology involves us in a profound paradox: Our action is morally permissible only up until the point we act and bring about unintended consequences. We are moral only up to the moment we act in a supposedly moral way. Like utilitarianism, deontology does not deal well with unintended consequences.

A Morality of Care

A morality of care emphasizes that human beings are interdependent. We are embedded selves, not free floating atoms. A care morality enjoins us to act in ways that honor and develop healthy relationships. Espoused primarily by women psychologists and feminists, a morality of care is not rule- or maxim-based. On the contrary, many women view rules with suspicion, because precepts are often laid down and enforced by those in power. The powerful typically are not very sensitive to the needs and concerns of those whom they are subjecting to their rules and policies. Moreover, rule-making tends to extol autonomy, logic, and rationality at the expense of inter-dependence and feeling. For these reasons, a morality of care stresses not rules but rather the cultivation of empathy, sympathy, trust, and other states or sensibilities that enable people to co-exist in mutually nurturing ways. In the words of Carol Gilligan (who was one of the first to propose the idea of a distinctively female morality of care), the

> moral imperative . . . [for] women is an injunction to care, a responsibility to discern and alleviate the "real and recognizable trouble" of this world. For men, the moral imperative appears rather as an injunction to respect the rights of others and thus to protect from interference the rights to life and self-fulfillment. . . . The standard of moral judgment that informs [women's] assessment of self is a standard of relationship. . . . Morality is seen by . . . women as arising from the experience of connection and is conceived as a problem of inclusion rather than one of balancing claims.[5]

Since the care morality's focus is on sensibility rather than rules, it is, in theory, more flexible than rule- or maxim-based moralities. It asks us to think about the larger effects of our actions on all people with whom we are in relationship. We are not locked into rigid, rational rules but can use our imagination to make various possible effects present to us. This freedom may help us discern unanticipated consequences.

The more empathetic we become, the more we will be able to view the world from other people's perspectives, thereby transcending our limited egoistic perspective. Indeed, if we are really serious about developing our empathy, we will cultivate a habit of reaching out and listening to people whom we may inadvertently victimize. Bernard Yack puts the point well:

> The significance that others find in our words and deeds tends to increase in proportion to the amount of power we have over their fate. What may seem to be a casual expression or an inconsequential indulgence can, and often does, have tremendous consequences for the less powerful individuals affected by such an action. We can, of course, make an effort to be sensitive to the unintended consequences of seemingly inconsequential actions. But, given our lack of omniscience, no one can recognize all of these consequences of her actions. Thus a whole range of harmful consequences will be apparent only to those whom they victimize. We will learn about these harmful consequences only if we listen to the voices of the individuals who feel victimized by our words and actions. These individuals may frequently look for victimizers even when none exist; but they also have insights into the harmful consequences of public actions we can get from no other source.[6]

This concern for victims has prompted some thinkers to

argue that we need to structure political institutions so as to ensure that marginalized groups are better represented in political forums and debates, a suggestion I will revisit in the next chapter.

A final point in favor of the care morality: It insists that, since we are born and die as relational selves, we have no choice but to remain engaged with and concerned about others throughout our entire lives. The morality implicitly requires that we monitor the consequences of our choices for as long as these choices impact our family, neighbors, and members of the larger community. In this respect, this morality could be said to be more sensitive to unfolding, unintended consequences than utilitarian or deontological moralities, which require us to focus on a single choice, render judgment on that choice, and then move on to the next issue.

That, then, is the good news about the care morality. The bad news is that, in practice, this morality, like utilitarianism and deontology, has difficulty both identifying and coping with unintended consequences. Since it so enthusiastically endorses the embedded self and recommends engrossing ourselves in friendships and familial relationships, it tends to overlook the many ways in which the community (including the family and religious groups) may oppress individuals (e.g., domestic violence; unequal allocation and valuation of housework and childcare). One unintended consequence of the care morality itself is that it undervalues a person's right to exit voluntarily from situations that he or she finds exploitive. Yet such a right is often the only recourse an individual may have for escaping from abusive relations. The morality risks locking us into relationships with brutes who are said to be part of our relational self.

While emphasizing the need for dialogue, proponents of this morality paradoxically proceed by unilaterally defining what they mean by "care." They would have us show concern for persons. But the morality's defenders, by and large, have forgotten about the need to care for dialogue. It is through respectful and truth-oriented dialogue that we can hope to learn about each other, discover our prejudices, identify our teleopathies, establish shared priorities, and reach compromises among competing claims put forth by those who want to receive care. By neglecting the importance of dialogue, the care morality veers toward something potentially quite dangerous. As advocates for the disabled have observed, a cared for person may not regard the caregiver's "care" as helpful or desirable. As Yack emphasizes, an empathic imagination will take us only so far. We may unknowingly wrongly imagine another person's perspective or feelings. If we are to have any chance of avoiding unintended consequences harmful to others, we need the hard reality check provided by free, respectful, and inclusive dialogue. That dialogue must somehow be institutionalized in our politics and daily practices. To date, most versions of the care morality have paid little or no attention to such conditions for such dialogue or to concrete practices that develop mindfulness.[7]

Virtue Morality

Unlike utilitarian, deontological and care moralities, virtue-based morality explicitly acknowledges that unintended consequences exist and can be problematic. The possibility of such consequences shapes what the virtue moralist Aristotle has to say about friendship. The virtuous person is someone who has good friends and who acts as a good friend to others. Aristotle's discussion of friendship implies that, even if a friend were unwittingly to harm us, we would readily forgive this friend if we ourselves are virtuous. The virtuous person becomes angry and terminates a friendship only when the friend has intentionally set out to inflict harm. Friendship among the virtuous has a built-in expansiveness precisely because those possessing *phronesis* or practical wisdom realize that our world is the sort of place where, as the T-shirt so pithily puts it, "shit happens." We human beings control only some events and have far less power than we like to pretend, in part because so many of our actions and policies have unintended, unforeseeable effects. That being so, a virtue morality asks us to cut each other some slack.

We would expect, then, that (1) a morality of virtue would acknowledge the existence of both historical contingencies and unintended consequences; and that (2) it would distinguish between foreseeable and unforeseeable unintended consequences, holding us accountable only for the former. Aristotle makes both of these claims. He contends that we generally are not to blame for chance events (i.e., historical contingencies) or unintended consequences.

Only in the case where a consequence of our act could have been foreseen by us if we had proceeded with greater care and thoughtfulness do we deserve to be held responsible for any harm we have caused. Although we may not have intended the harm, we remain responsible for having made ourselves into careless people. If we are ignorant of possible outcomes because we are drunk or enraged; because we failed to learn from past experience; or because we were indifferent to the welfare of others, then the fault lies with us. Aristotle reminds us that we are the "moving principle" in such cases and so could have behaved differently. Whenever acts are initiated by us, and whenever the consequences of these actions are within our power to bring about or to refrain from causing, then these deeds qualify as voluntary.

A virtue morality holds us responsible for all of our voluntary acts and their consequences. True, the alcoholic may not know what he is doing. Still, it was, Aristotle insists, once open to the drunkard not to drink and to become an alcoholic. Although the drunk driver may not have intended to kill a pedestrian, she voluntarily did so because it was foreseeable that she might have an accident when driving under the influence. If we indulge our anger when someone cuts us off on the highway, then we voluntarily experience road rage. It does not take a genius to know that aggressive driving is dangerous. If we fail to foresee the possibility of a wreck, our ignorance is self-caused or self-induced. We should have roused our intellect to consider the likely effects of permitting ourselves to become so angry. Despite the fact that we may not have intended or planned the wreck caused by our aggressive driving, we voluntarily caused the accident and are thus justly held to be responsible for the damage. Similar reasoning would apply to foreseeable unintended consequences involving adaptations to rules or policy changes (e.g., investment banks engaging in balance sheet games in response to more stringent capital requirements imposed by the Fed). If regulators and policy-makers fail to consider foreseeable unintended consequences, a virtue moralist would argue that they deserve to be blamed for this failure of prudence. These parties' ignorance was self-caused and remediable.

In other cases, though, our ignorance is excusable. If we cause unintended harm because we are ignorant of some factor or feature, and if our ignorance of that factor is neither self-caused nor of the sort that we could easily have remedied if we had taken more care, then we should not be accused of voluntarily producing harm. Aristotle carves out a class of acts done "by reason of ignorance." Acts falling into this second category are those with completely unforeseeable, unimagined consequences. A fencer with a defective foil who accidentally kills his opponent thinks he is engaged in a competition, not a fight to the death. As long as he did not know that his foil was defective, his killing of his opponent was the result of irremediable ignorance and should be judged involuntary. His act is more of a pure accident or a historical contingency than a plotted course and, therefore, does not deserve our censure. The regulators who created securitized assets to deal with the S&L crisis could not have known that they were setting into motion an entire wave of securitizations that would bring huge risks in its wake. In this sense, their action with its unintended adaptive response was involuntary, and involuntary actions are, Aristotle contends, to be pitied or pardoned, not praised or blamed.[8]

An Aristotelian virtue morality has the merit of explicitly recognizing a class of genuinely involuntary deeds. His idea of friendship coupled with forgiveness gives us some scope for coping with both unintended adaptive responses and with historical contingencies. Yet, although a morality of virtue is better equipped to cope with unintended consequences than utilitarian or Kantian moralities, it struggles to deal with this class of effects. A morality of virtue underestimates just how often unforeseeable unintended consequences occur. Jonas is quite right: Virtue moralities are "accustomed to dealing with human action that [falls] within well-defined and familiar parameters."[9] Aristotle clearly believes that actions are rarely caused by involuntary, non-remediable excusable ignorance. At the beginning of Book 3 of his work on morality, he methodically demonstrates how actions assumed to be involuntary are, in reality, voluntary. Although we may not like the alternatives we face, we nonetheless make a choice when we opt for one course in preference to another. Even some deeds done under extreme torture are, Aristotle suggests, voluntary.[10] Moreover, although we occasionally act from ignorance, our ignorance is usually self-caused and remediable. In other words, our ignorance is voluntary and deserves to be blamed and censured. In a dig at his mentor Plato, Aristotle observes that surely no one could fail to know who he is.[11] In Aristotle's view, we are not justified in arguing that an act of ours derives from a failure in self-knowledge. Plato's Socrates was wrong to suggest that we do not comprehend who we are and do not understand our motivations or intentions.

In summary, virtue-based morality treats the vast majority of our actions as voluntary. From one point of view, this approach is commendable. By holding us responsible for our deeds and choices and for the character that develops through the actions we initiate, Aristotle tries to get us to proceed more thoughtfully and to refine our power to make prudent judgments. If we come to understand that we have more freedom than most people believe, then we are more likely to exercise greater control over our character and to become ever more autonomous and free.

This character-building approach, however, minimizes the threat unintended consequences pose to our freedom. Virtue moralities make us more masters of fate than we actually are. Even when we try to act mindfully, we inevitably discover that our choices produce unintended and possibly undesirable consequences. To the extent that these consequences are genuinely unforeseeable and exactly opposite to what we had hoped to accomplish, we find ourselves thwarted and our happiness diminished. A morality of virtue informs us which choices and deeds merit blame, but offers few constructive means for helping us avoid (or, at least, minimize) unintended consequences. In addition, Aristotle's discussion of unintended consequences does not focus on foreseeable or unforeseeable reactions to new laws or policies by large segments of the population. His virtue morality concentrates more on individual passions and on poorly reasoned choices than on adaptive social responses.

Given that none of the standard moral theories enables us to grapple well with unintended consequences, how should we proceed if we wish to act more ethically? To that question I now turn.

4

POSSIBLE ETHICAL REMEDIES

If our common moral frameworks do not enable us to cope well with unintended consequences, how then should we deal with them? Is there a way for us to act more responsibly and to minimize the number and impact of unintended consequences?

The analysis of the previous chapter suggests that a rule-based or more algorithmic moral approach is not going to be of much use. Instead, we should concentrate on improving our ability to discern possible effects of deeds, policies, interventions, and laws. That means adopting structures, perspectives, understandings, and practices that foster mindfulness and that bring multiple intelligences to bear on problems at hand. Deontology and utilitarianism assume that a lone individual can unilaterally arrive at the ethically correct course of action. However, that assumption is not warranted. No single person has sufficient experience and imagination to anticipate and grapple with the diverse unintended consequences that so often result from human choices. We will fare better if we collectively strive to develop discernment and prudence and to evolve various components of what might be thought of as an ethic of preparedness or an ethic of attentiveness.[1]

There is no one-size-fits-all remedy for avoiding unintended consequences. Just as there are three types of causes of such consequences—worldly, practical, and psychological—so, too, are there three corresponding types of remedies. These three approaches can increase awareness of possible unintended consequences and thus enhance our ability to ward off outcomes deemed hostile to our individual and collective well-being. By adopting these measures, we may reasonably hope to become more concerned, caring, and prudent. These remedies, though, do not guarantee that we will be able to head-off even those threats we successfully foresee. Sometimes discernment comes too late in the day.

Worldly Remedies

If we wish to minimize unintended consequences caused by the world's complexity and diversity; by our pervasive "Master of the Universe" and Newtonian mindsets (which are ill-adapted to the complex social and ecological realities facing us); and by our ever greater ability to cause massive and possibly irreparable harm to the world, we should seek out more helpful worldviews and adopt structures and institutions better suited for helping us identify and address these consequences.

Adopting an Ecological Perspective

As we saw in Chapter 2, many ecologists regard global laws with suspicion. Regularities, they argue, may exist but tend to be valid only for narrow niches. For example, although it may be true that the melting of glaciers will lead to rising sea levels in some parts of the world, the water may actually fall dramatically in other areas, even at locations closest to the melting glaciers. As the Alaskan glaciers have receded, the land has risen. Ice is heavy, and as it disappears, the land springs back. The up-thrusting land, in turn, is causing the seas around Alaska to retreat at an accelerating rate.

> The geology is complex, but it boils down to this: Relieved of billions of tons of glacial weight, the land has risen much as a cushion regains its shape after someone gets up from a couch. The land is ascending so fast that the rising seas—a ubiquitous by-product of global warming—cannot keep pace. As a result, the relative sea level is falling, at a rate "among the highest ever recorded," according to a 2007 report by a panel of experts. . . . Greenland and a few other places have experienced similar effects from widespread glacial melting that began more than 200 years ago, geologists say. But, they say, the effects are more noticeable in and near Juneau, where most glaciers are retreating 30 feet a year or more.
>
> As a result, the region faces unusual environmental challenges. As the sea level falls relative to the land, water tables fall, too, and streams and wetlands dry out. Land is emerging from the water to replace the lost wetlands, shifting property boundaries and causing people to argue about who owns the

acreage and how it should be used. And meltwater carries the sediment scoured long ago by the glaciers to the coast, where it clouds the water and silts up once-navigable channels.[2]

This example illustrates niche behavior as the exact opposite of what experts forecast would happen. Theories of how global warming will proceed need to be supplemented with careful observation; environmental "solutions" should be embraced with extreme caution. It would be wise for us to cultivate a skeptical attitude toward sweeping generalizations about what will or will not happen if we perform some act (e.g., adding huge quantities of carbon dioxide to the earth's atmosphere). The Newtonian mindset has played us false in the past and will continue to do so. A more humble, ecological perspective based on close observations of niche behavior would serve us better. Such a stance would alert us to specific developments in particular niches and make us more hesitant to make or to accept grand prognostications about benefits to be realized through programs, laws, and initiatives aimed at addressing one problem or another.

Reconciling Ourselves to Muddling Through

The political scientist Charles Lindblom was among the first modern theorists to warn against too heavy reliance on scientific theories, especially by social scientists. He rejected what he termed the "root" method of decision-making.[3] The root method begins by stating the problem, identifying objectives, prioritizing values, and then evaluating options for attaining these objectives. This approach (which defenders modeled on the "hard" sciences of physics and chemistry) makes many of the Newtonian assumptions I have been criticizing. In particular, the root method assumes that what has worked in the past will work again in the future (i.e., that global rules exist and are valid) and that we can somehow comprehensively grasp all relevant options and identify every relevant fact. The hallmarks of the root method are "clarity of objective, explicitness of evaluation, a high degree of comprehensiveness of overview, and wherever possible, quantification of values for mathematical analysis."[4]

Lindblom doubted the soundness of the scientific root approach. He believed that people didn't actually make decisions in this systematic, quasi-mechanical way. Nor could they do so, because they lacked the time and money to perform this sort of analysis. Furthermore, people usually disagree on which values are most relevant when it comes to addressing an issue and thus cannot reach a consensus on the right value hierarchy. Lindblom noted that even Charles Hitch, the then head of the Economics Division of the Rand Corporation (celebrated at the time for its scientific systems approach), believed that the root approach was of limited applicability and value. Hitch conceded that, although the simple explicit models favored by operations researchers are helpful in, say, analyzing factors affecting traffic flow on a bridge, these models will not be able to capture and represent the relevant factors affecting far more complex choices such as foreign policy decisions.[5]

Lindblom favored a "branch" method for arriving at decisions when it came to thinking about complex policy issues. The branch method proceeds by small degrees and incremental steps, working from present arrangements and making only modest changes to policies. We should use what we know worked in the past but be prepared to revise our thinking in new contexts. Indeed, we should imitate nature, which evolves new organisms by "adding a new level of programming on top of an already well-established set of instructions, [with] each species" containing a "strong foundation of time-tested DNA sequences. . . . [In this simple way] nature transmits the experience and wisdom bestowed by ancient life to her progeny."[6] This naturalistic method—which Lindblom thought was the approach most used by practitioners, policy-makers, and public administrators—recognizes that we typically confront poorly defined alternatives, lack complete information about our options, do not fully know what the possible consequences of different options might be, lack consensus on which values should govern our decisions, and operate with limited time, skills, and resources.

Political scientists and management whiz kids heaped scorn upon Lindblom when he first proposed this method of conservative incrementalism. But the overview of unintended consequences sketched in the earlier chapters suggests that Lindblom was quite right to urge restraint and to resist the sweeping overhauls being pushed by supposed experts. Experts tend to ignore human complexity and adaptability and to overlook just how different the various ecological niches of our world are. Which social objective we will prefer depends upon the conditions of choice and the nature of available options.[7]

It is time for us to live with the reality that we must continually rethink our values and priorities as we encounter novel problems. The branch approach, far from being some second-best method, possesses substantial advantages:

> Policy is not made once and for all; it is made and re-made endlessly. Policy-making is a process of successive approximation to some desired objectives in which what is desired itself continues to change under reconsideration. . . . Neither social scientists, nor politicians, nor public administrators know enough about the social world to avoid repeated error in predicting the consequences of policy moves. *A wise policy-maker consequently expects that his policies will achieve only part of what he hopes and at the same time will produce unanticipated consequences he would have preferred to avoid.* If he proceeds through a succession of incremental changes, he avoids serious lasting mistakes in several ways.
>
> In the first place, past sequences of policy steps have given him knowledge about the probable consequences of further similar steps. Second, he need not attempt big jumps toward his goals that would require predictions beyond his or anyone else's knowledge, because he never expects his policy to be a final resolution of a problem. . . . Third, he is in effect able to test his previous predictions as he moves on to each further step (italics mine).[8]

Recognize the Imperative of Responsibility

Embracing an ecological perspective structured around conservative incrementalism is a step in the right direction. The perspective should be supplemented with Jonas' "imperative of responsibility." Jonas, recall, contends that we maintain ourselves in the world, by it, and against it. Given that we may act in a way that leads to our extermination, human beings have an interest in being, to use Jonas' word, "concerned" for the world. Jonas asks us always to remember how precarious life is. He invites us to subject ourselves to one over-riding ethical demand or imperative: "Act so that the effects of your action are compatible with the permanence of genuine human life."[9] Although this imperative of responsibility does not, in itself, have much content, it does focus our attention on just high how the stakes are for us when we make choices.

Jonas' maxim requires us to develop habits of mindfulness and attention. By training ourselves to emphasize this maxim in our public political and educational discourse, we can perhaps avoid some egregious outcomes. Adherence to the imperative of responsibility would make us more wary of rushing to embrace the latest technologies and adopting large-scale technological interventions as solutions to problems. Jonas' imperative is especially relevant to the current push to engage in geoengineering. This new field proposes to lessen the impact of global warming by using man-made techniques to cool the planet. Two techniques are receiving serious attention: (1) sending up balloons or artillery shells designed to inject massive amounts of sulfates into the atmosphere; and (2) creating artificial clouds by pumping sea water into the air. The sulfate technique seeks to imitate volcanic explosions, which are known to create huge clouds of sulfur dioxide dust that can lower the earth's temperature dramatically. The second approach aims at increasing the cloud layer so that the larger number and greater thickness of clouds will reflect more sunlight, thereby lowering the earth's temperature.[10]

Blithe talk of geoengineering should give us pause. Either of these techniques might well produce horrific unintended consequences more worrisome than the warming they seek to ameliorate. Sulfates from past volcanic explosions have damaged the ozone layer. Sulfate injections might result in higher skin cancer rates and other health problems. How would they affect the rain cycle? Would reduced sunlight make it difficult to rely on solar power as a substitute for fossil fuels? How often would we have to perform these injections? And what would happen if we stopped them? Would the earth's surface temperature then shoot up even higher? We would not know until after we used the technique. Creating cloud cover could have similarly devastating results. There might be sustained downpours in areas already projected to flood if global warming causes sea levels to rise. Would the losing countries view these technological interventions by the developed world as acts of aggression and respond by declaring war? The treatment in this case could be worse than the disease.

Jonas' astute observation that so-called experts are not especially prescient is apropos. Even to propose such large-scale interventions may be a violation of the imperative of responsibility. Instead of devising dramatic engineering responses, we might be better off muddling through, making small rather than dramatic interventions, and doing so only after extensive and inclusive public debates about possible benefits and dangers of these micro-adjustments.

Embrace Federalism and Subsidiarity

Years ago when I was a student at Oxford University studying political theory and institutions, my very British college tutor groused, "I don't know how you Americans do it. Your political system is not rational. Yet somehow you seem to muddle through." At the time, I did not realize that he was alluding to (and deprecating) Lindblom's work. His comment stuck with me not because I understood the reference but because it was both condescending and true. Americans are blessed with a complex federal system that grants power to local communities and states as well as to the national government. This system of matrixed and balanced powers is designed to force citizens from all walks of life to talk with each other. Sometimes these discussions are more rants than civil exchanges. Not all shared information is equally good. Nonetheless, information does get disseminated. For those people who are paying attention, the federal system provides an opportunity to learn details that can be factored into the making of decisions. Americans don't just muddle along. Usually we muddle through rather brilliantly, especially when these conversations give us a sense of the range of possible intended and unintended consequences of proposed acts.

Listening to our fellow citizens is not an especially systematic practice, but the payoff is potentially huge. By shifting from relying on supposed experts to paying greater attention to what our peers at the state and local levels are observing and talking about, we increase the odds that we will perceive salient differences among various cultural niches. Appreciating and supporting federalism is one way to cultivate a more ecological mindset and to encourage use of a Lindblomian branch method in policy-making and reforms.

A federalist mindset is helpful in another way. Local people typically have the best sense of neighborhood conditions. America's founding fathers consciously adopted what the Catholic Church refers to as the "principle of subsidiarity." The papal encyclical "Quadragesimo Anno" proclaims, "It is grave injustice, a grave evil and a disturbance of right order for a large and higher organization to arrogate to itself functions that can be performed efficiently by smaller and lower bodies. . . ."[11] In other words, regimes should practice reverse delegation, allowing citizens a chance to make choices and learn from their mistakes by means of a system in which local knowledge can be brought to bear by those who are most directly affected by political decisions. Although we cannot eliminate the complexity of the world, we can, by drawing upon our neighbors' knowledge embedded in diverse perspectives, better anticipate and think through potentially dire consequences of proposed courses of action.

This knowledge can be used not only when drafting local ordinances but also when thinking about national legislation applicable to very different states. Our forefathers believed that a federal system would enable representatives to educate each other:

> Were the interests and affairs of each individual State perfectly simple and uniform, a knowledge of them in one part would involve a knowledge of them in every other, and the whole State might be competently represented by a single member taken from any part of it. On a comparison of the different States together, we find a great dissimilarity in their laws, and in many other circumstances connected with the objects of federal legislation, with all of which the federal representatives ought to have some acquaintance. Whilst a few representatives, therefore, from each State, may bring with them a due knowledge of their own State, every representative will have much information to acquire concerning all the other States.[12]

When officials from each state share their regional wisdom, the national legislative body is more advantageously positioned to evaluate policies and laws. Instead of representing narrow interests, representatives can further the good of the whole. At the same time, the federal system provides a check on local prejudices and biases. Town and state passions often run high. National laws and uniform regulations coupled with a two-tiered national legislative body help insure that representatives and officials do not fall prey to ill-judged positions adopted in the heat of the moment.

Adopt Institutional Arrangements that Recognize Our
Individual Ignorance and Better Protect the Marginalized

The "Master of the Universe" mentality, which Hans Jonas took to be symptomatic of the modern world, is an instance of hubris, the sin of pretending that we know more than we really do. Humility is the best antidote to hubris. We need to admit that, in fact, we do not know everything, and to ask for input from people who operate outside of our chosen fields and industries. Outsiders provide a fresh perspective. President Franklin Delano Roosevelt would query Oval Office visitors about issues he was facing. Visitors from Kansas or Vermont might be asked about defense issues. FDR would quiz the agriculture secretary on what the man thought about the value of the gold standard. In this way, he sought to incorporate many and varied perspectives into his thinking. He wanted fresh thinking from outside the capitol cocoon.

Boards of directors have long appointed outside dir-ectors in an effort to institutionalize "thinking outside the box." Outside directors sometimes ask the best questions. Their ignorance of details and of corporate history, politics, and presuppositions allows them cut through to the key issue. As Peter Drucker sagely observes, "Ignorance is not such a bad thing if one knows how to use it . . . and all managers [and knowledge workers] must learn how to do this. You must frequently approach problems with your ignorance; not what you think you know from past experience, because not infrequently, what you think you know is wrong."[13]

Talking with and listening well to a diverse group frequently is better than consulting self-styled experts. James Surowiecki has documented the wisdom of crowds. He recounts numerous instances where the many have proven to be smarter than the few. For example, the statistician Francis Galton was surprised to find that, when he averaged the guesses a crowd at the county fair made regarding an ox's weight, this collective average was closer to the animal's actual butchered weight than any individual guess made by cattle experts.[14] Crowds are wisest when members have local knowledge (which buttresses my earlier point about subsidiarity), when the collective is diverse (FDR's insight), and when members form their judgments independently (i.e., when they avoid groupthink). Under these conditions, consulting with many people improves our chances of foreseeing perverse or undesirable side effects of a proposed policy or law. Representatives and policy-makers should consider how better to tap into the citizenry's collective wisdom. Perhaps more town hall meetings or online conversations with constituents would help decision-makers zero in on foreseeable but unintended consequences.

People at the margin of public debate especially suffer from unintended consequences. They are virtually invisible. Their concerns are not heard. Those of us living in democracies should take seriously Iris Young's suggestion that we rethink group representation within government in order to ensure that the concerns of disadvantaged groups get heard. Sometimes a lone voice crying in the wilderness is not enough. The marginalized may need to reach a critical mass in order to have any real power to shape their destiny and to get the majority of representatives (be they local, state, or national) to heed unintended harms likely to be inflicted on those at the fringes of society. We would have to tinker with these group representations as we worked with them. Nor ought we to proceed naively or in haste. Any adopted remedy likely would bring in its wake more unintended consequences. Increased representation of smaller groups might lead to political instability and make closure difficult if fragmentation made it harder to build coalitions. It might also entrench today's minorities at the expense of future minorities. Demographics are changing rapidly. Today's minorities may be tomorrow's majorities.[15] Still, experimenting with ways to permit minorities to attain critical mass may be the relatively best way to bring concerns out into the open and to get us deliberating about how to protect the welfare of all community members.

Devising better ways to hear from the wide diversity of people within our own country would give us insight into the thinking of citizens of other countries. That increased understanding, in turn, could enable us to minimize some of the unintended outcomes that occur because—as Herodotus saw—we do not correctly interpret the actions and speech of those who belong to other cultures.

Practical Remedies

These, then, are a few alternative worldviews and related institutional arrangements that might make us more careful and thoughtful in our approach to change. Are there any specific practices, though, that will help us better cope with the unintended consequences arising from practical freedom itself? Adjusting our mindsets and governmental structures is a step in the right direction. But we need as well to rethink the nature of judgment and consider adopting specific practices that would refine both individual and collective judgment and get us to care more about our acts by making us feel more responsible for them.

Expand the Public Sphere In Order to Discover the Universal in the Particular

We obviously cannot stop acting and certainly do not want to renounce the freedom at the heart of our humanity. Arendt proposes that we cope with unintended consequences of human freedom by expanding the public sphere and encouraging ever-wider participation in debates. The Arendtian public sphere has two dimensions: It is both the space in which community members appear to each other and are able to act together by means of speech and persuasion; and the relatively permanent common world of institutions, practices, and settings in which we bring new things into being. This public sphere cannot exist if citizens insist on leading private lives. It is not enough for us to come out once every two or four years to cast a vote. We must meet and argue with each other on a regular basis. Only by participating in the space of public debate and contest can we realize ourselves as free and equal beings and simultaneously improve our judgments:

The power of [sound] judgment rests on a potential agreement with others, and the thinking process which is active
in judging something is not, like the thought process of
pure reasoning, a dialogue between me and myself, but finds
itself always and primarily . . . in an anticipated communication with others with whom I know I must finally come
to some agreement. From this potential agreement such
judgment derives its specific validity. This means . . . that
such judgment must liberate itself from the "subjective
private conditions," that is from the idiosyncrasies which
naturally determine the outlook of each individual in his
privacy and are legitimate as long as they are only privately
held opinions but which are not fit to enter the marketplace, and lack all validity in the public realm. And
this enlarged way of thinking, which as judgment knows
how to transcend its individual limitation, cannot function
in strict isolation or solitude; it needs the presence of
others . . . whose perspective it must take into consideration,
and without whom it never has the opportunity to operate
at all.[16]

Arendt's central insight is that more information *per
se* does not guarantee better judgment. Our judgments
improve only when our effort to accommodate diverse perspectives forces us *to find the universal in the particular*.
As we seek potential agreement with our conversation
partners, we become less inclined to subsume the individual case under some inapplicable or outmoded universal.
Our judgments become more genuinely objective and
nuanced as we ponder an array of arresting anecdotes and

arguments advanced by a wide variety of individuals who are thinking about highly specific problems.

This process of persuasive debate and consultation with other people never ends. We never solve our practical problems once and for all. Through dialogue, however, we gain a sense of power and self-worth. In addition, discussions with fellow citizens forge a sense of solidarity, alerting us to our collective power at the same time as they reveal our individual blind spots. Only in direct democracy do we come to see ourselves as what Thomas Jefferson termed "participators in government." Arendt would have us be a bit suspicious of our elected representatives. Yes, the local knowledge of representatives, the separation of powers, and a federalist system aid in the refinement of judgment. There is, however, always a danger when others speak for us. Representation tempts elected officials to think of themselves as superior to those they govern. Since no one is a master of highly unpredictable human action, this hubristic belief in superiority is a perilous thing. Ideological representatives may decide they know exactly which system or set of rules will promote collective welfare. Instead of ceding too much power to representatives, we should continue to "muddle through" by means of widespread participation of citizens in local councils, town and condo association meetings, unions, etc.

The Internet and new electronic media have the potential to function as forums for the discussion of important issues. Some chat rooms and blogs operate primarily as spaces for ranting or, in extreme cases, spewing hatred. In many cases, though, blogs and postings have enabled thoughtful people outside of Washington, D.C. and the established media to enter the public sphere and to voice arguments and concerns worthy of being considered. Although the Internet definitely has a dark side, it also offers a way to realize Arendt's suggestion that we expand the public sphere so as to hone judgment with a view to finding the universal in the particular. We should continue to experiment with ways to bring civil and focused debates over policies and reforms to an ever-wider group of citizens. President Obama's efforts in 2008 to establish a clearinghouse of ideas on how to improve government and to create a public interest wiki maintained by citizens at large was an experiment in this vein.

Promote the Return of a Craft Ethic

In Chapter 3, I criticized virtue-based morality for failing to grasp how widespread and frequent unintended consequences are. This morality's marked tendency to view actions as fully within our control is a defect. On the other hand, the morality's insistence that we bear responsibility for our choices is not completely mistaken. If we do not feel that we have any responsibility for what we bring about, we are not likely to care for others or for the world. In this respect, Aristotle was correct to believe that we can refine our judgment only if we attend to how we frame situations and construe our own agency. If we *think* we are entirely at the mercy of external forces, then over time, we will become less able to act freely. We will be buffeted hither and thither by external forces precisely because we have not devoted any energy to discovering where we do have options and do have room to maneuver. One might say: We are only as free as we think we are. The question then becomes: How can we get people to think of themselves as more free to determine their fate? In particular, how can we get people to care enough about what they are doing to think through effects of their deeds?

One step toward improving judgments in the workplace is to qualify Arendt's sharp and dangerously sweeping distinction between making and acting. Arendt elevates action above making because a doer is, she thinks, free, while a maker is subject to the constraints imposed by the product he or she is making. Arendt forgets that constraint is not necessarily the enemy of freedom. Musicians have long understood that the best innovators are those who have learned the rules of composition and the limits of their instruments. Artists are most free to improvise and to "create the world anew" when they are the most disciplined. The great sitar player Ravi Shankar writes that it "is only after many long and extensive years of *sadhana* (dedicated practice and discipline) under the guidance of one's guru and his blessings, that the artist is empowered to put *prana* (the breath of life) into a *raga* (an Indian sitar piece)."[17]

When people in the trades, arts, and crafts submit to the discipline of what they produce or service—be it a clay pot, motorcycle, or a raga—, they are living a craft ethic. There was a robust craft ethic in Europe and America back when workmen took pride in their individual products (which were frequently customized) and delighted in signing their work. The craft ethic lives on in Japan where local authorities and the national government annually honor master woodworkers, ceramicists, weavers, etc. In the West, the development of the modern assembly line resulted in workers no longer feeling any personal connection with what they produced. Consequently, they had no incentive to attend to what they were doing or to care about how their behavior was affecting the larger world. Individuals who do not even bother with trying to judge well do not become adept at anticipating foreseeable unintended consequences nor at imagining ways to cope with any unforeseeable outcomes that may occur. So as workers relinquished their craft, their powers of discernment suffered.

By contrast, individuals who practice craft in a context in which they control the conditions of production typically feel the weight of personal responsibility. In his lovely essay "The Case for Working with Your Hands," motorcycle mechanic Matthew Crawford describes the anxiety he felt when he accidentally dropped a feeler gauge into a customer's Kawasaki's crankcase.[18] The bike was almost new. If he could not get the gauge out, he would have to face the customer and explain the damage he had wrought. This sort of pressure is a daily fact of life for those who work in the crafts: "Catastrophe [is] an always present possibility."[19] Pressure concentrates the practitioner's attention on the task at hand. And the fact that the artisan alone is doing the work means that "the core experience is one of individual responsibility. . . ."[20] This experience is reinforced by the direct interaction between artisans and the customers they serve. Unlike business managers who endeavor to deflect personal responsibility by not assuming owner-ship for their actions, craftspeople find it far harder to evade accountability for what they do or fail to accomplish.

Assuming responsibility makes sense, because the chain of cause and effect is relatively clearer in the crafts than in other activities. Knowledge workers—e.g., business people or politicians—may have little sense of accomplishment at the end of the workday and almost no awareness of whom they have affected by their choices. Responsibility, if it exists at all, is diffuse. Craft practitioners, by contrast, must understand how their decisions will affect the quilt they are making or the wood they are sawing. Each day they use this cause–effect nexus to accomplish their goals. And, at the end of the day, they know whether they played every note, completed twenty quilt squares, or finished the customer's repair on time. Craft practitioners grasp that they them-selves are a cause. They instinctively know that they are what Aristotle calls an *archē* or an originator of voluntary deeds.

Woodworkers or motorcycle mechanics are not so know-ledgeable about causes and consequences that they never make mistakes. On the contrary, disaster always looms, in large part because the source of problems encountered may not be immediately obvious. Figuring out the cause may involve actions (e.g., removing a bunch of rusted bolts on an engine cover in order to look into the machine) that introduce a new set of risks. The mechanic may trigger a host of additional complications if the bolts he is removing are stripped or break off. Over time craft practitioners become acutely aware that their "solutions" may create a whole new set of problems. It is not surprising that they evolve into rather cautious souls who shun rules and generalizations, preferring to use a version of Lindblom's branch method and to focus on idiosyncratic details of the matter at hand:

> [M]anuals tell you to be systematic in eliminating variables, presenting an idealized image of diagnostic work. But they never take into account the risks of working on old machines. So you put the manual away and consider the facts before you. You do this because ultimately you are responsible to the motorcycle and its owner, not to some procedure.[21]

Caution (coupled with a heightened awareness of the high stakes involved) begets humility.

Refined habits instilled by years of practice enable the practitioner to better foresee unintended consequences falling into the class of anticipatable effects. How so? Artisans learn to pay attention to what they are doing. Wary of introducing new difficulties, they proceed conservatively, "measuring twice, cutting once." Since they are directly accountable to end users (who may refuse to pay the bill if the work is done poorly!), and since they generally can see the immediate consequences of their action, they are extra sensitive to causes and effects. Knowing that they may be wrong, they do not rush in, but pause to consider possible undesirable effects of their interventions. This habitual way of thinking increases the likelihood that this class of doers will anticipate some of the foreseeable unintended consequences of their choices.

What about unforeseeable unintended consequences? A craft ethic can help with these as well. Insofar as practicing a craft increases workers' alertness, they can more quickly spot emerging unintended consequences. The willingness and ability of a practitioner of a craft or trade to treat each encounter with material as a new situation calling for imaginative reasoning creates a more flexible mind. It develops the practitioner's ability to play with hypotheses and to entertain previously unconsidered possibilities. Flexibility of mind is an asset when it comes to coping with consequences that were not foreseen but that are occurring nonetheless.

A related point: As Crawford notes, in political and academic life, causes and their effects are not as apparent as they are in crafts. Our body politic will be healthier if we have some citizens whose creative activity and whose visible effect on the material they shape daily reminds them that they possess agency and power. By promoting a sense of responsibility among practitioners, a craft ethic keeps people engaged with and committed to their actions. Having such a sense of agency is important precisely because the presence of unintended consequences can alienate us from our deeds. It can diffuse responsibility to the point where we cease to feel any connection with the effects we are producing, be they intentional or inadvertent. Such diffusion is a genuine threat in this era of knowledge workers, so we should foster practices that cultivate our sense of ourselves as responsible agents whose critical and perceptual abilities can be developed and perfected. Craftsmanship bestows another benefit. It instills in the practitioner a sense that his or her work possesses intrinsic value, thereby reducing the feeling of inquietude that haunts modern workers in the West and drives them to seek peace through shopping. By checking our avidity and calming us down, a craft ethic may even make us better citizens.

Cultivating a craft ethic will not solve all of our woes. Such an ethic has dangers of its own. The scientists who built the atom bomb took pride in their work and were aware of how high the stakes were for them and for the country. It could be argued that they had a craft ethic of sort. Nevertheless, for the most part, they did not ask larger questions about the meaning and goodness of the Manhattan Project.[22] In this case, scientists' belief in universal laws (reinforced by a Master of the Universe mentality) led them to ponder primarily technical issues and to ignore the larger geo-political implications of their deeds. Nevertheless, returning to a craft ethic and funding robust vocational education programs would foster, I believe, greater awareness of our responsibility in, to, and for the world. It would sustain a sense that we are not merely at the mercy of external forces. Through discipline, we would begin to live as if we were free and that new habit would, in turn, breed a sense that we own our actions. We would care more for the world and such caring would make us more attentive to what we are doing. We would enter a virtuous circle of self-heightening sensitivity.

There is ample anecdotal evidence to support this view. The Total Quality Movement found that quality improved substantially after workers on assembly lines were empowered to stop the lines whenever they perceived a problem. Businesses that have reintroduced a craft ethic have been pleasantly surprised by the results:

> A friend was appointed manager of a small art-printing works. Shortly after his arrival he called the whole workforce together and told them that he was ashamed of the quality of much of the work that had been going out of the door. In the future, he told them, everyone who has worked on an order must sign their name on a slip that will go out with the order saying, "We are responsible for this work. We hope that you are pleased with it." "I expected a revolt," he said, "but instead they cheered." "We, too, have been ashamed of much of the work. But we thought that that was what you wanted—the lowest acceptable quality at the lowest cost. We are happy to sign our names, provided you supply us with the machines that allow us to do work to our standards."[23]

The manager agreed to these conditions and work quality and employee and customer satisfaction improved dramatically.

Use Planning Methods That Stimulate Probing Discussion

Not only structures and worldviews but also techniques need to be evaluated in terms of their power to assist us in anticipating unintended consequences. Planning Poker is a technique being used in software development to estimate the effort, risk, and amount of planning involved in a project. Developers typically have different ideas about what that project will entail. Technical employees' conception may diverge radically from the ideas of colleagues on the marketing or financial side of the business. Yet one group's concerns may not get voiced for a variety of reasons. Once the project has begun, it may be too late to incorporate and respond to concerns not shared earlier in the planning process. As a result, the project may fail to meet its stated goal or be plagued by unintended consequences. In Planning Poker, team members discuss the project plan and requirements. Then, as a way of reaching consensus on the scope of the project, the effort required, and the risk involved, the project manager asks team members to play a round of Planning Poker. Each person gets eleven cards numbered (0, ½, 1, 2, 3, 5, 8, 13, 20, 40, and 100). These numbers represent a scale of relative weight/concern. If a team member thinks that the task in question will require quite a lot of time or entail much risk, then he or she selects a higher number; less time and risk, a lower number. The choices are kept secret until all have picked their cards. The players throw down their chosen card at the same time. If there is a large disparity in numbers played, then more discussion is needed to unearth why some members think the task will be easy, while others believe it will be more difficult. In some cases, the team members may be interpreting the scope of the task description differently; in other instances, a participant may know of obstacles or factors ignored by others. Planning Poker helps insure that each team member's voice gets heard as part of the process to expose hidden complexities. Used by a skillful project manager, the technique stimulates participants to think more deeply and systematically about possible difficulties at the front end of a project.

Planning Poker resembles the Delphi method in which various group members respond to structured questions. A moderator synthesizes these answers and then feeds them back to the group members who respond again in light of what their peers have said. This method has been used successfully in business forecasting. Shankar Basu and Roger Schroeder found that the Delphi method was able to predict sales of a new product relatively well. This method had a 3–4% inaccuracy rate compared with 10–15% forecast errors using quantitative techniques.[24] The method works because group members feel challenged to refocus and refine their thinking after hearing input from other participants. Deferring judgment allows many ideas to be put on the table. Creativity is not stifled as it so often is when the pressure is on to reach an immediate assessment. In these respects, techniques such as Planning Poker and the Delphi method can aid in the identification of possible unintended consequences.

Create Community Brainstorming Forums

Urban planning is rife with unintended consequences. After many years of half-acre lot development, city planners finally began to realize that this type of urbanization virtually required people to build their lives around cars. Air pollution, increased demand for gas, and road congestion were but a few unenvisioned and unintended effects of half-lot development. Given the pervasiveness of undesired outcomes resulting from poor planning, it is no wonder that urban planners and community redevelopers have invented community brainstorming. This technique, like Planning Poker, is designed to identify upfront hitherto overlooked consequences.

Suppose urban planners are contemplating planting trees throughout the city. Planners write "Tree Planting" in the middle of a huge piece of paper. Then community members, in an open forum, write down possible impacts of this course of action. Positive effects may include increased heat absorption by trees, improved air and water quality, more elderly people willing to walk outside because of shade cover, etc. On the negative side, more trees may cause numerous power outages as branches fall on lines during ice storms, result in escalating city costs for pruning trees, and so on. After getting this input, group facilitators direct participants to consider consequences of these impacts. Although this iterative process does not solve all development issues, it surfaces possible problems early in the planning process and pinpoints areas where more research may be needed.[25]

Plan for Unintended Consequences

Another practical step for coping with the uncertainty inherent in free human action involves expanding the Kantian idea of respect for persons to include planning for unintended consequences. An action that incorporates such planning should count as more respectful than one that does not. The idea of planning for unintended consequences is not as far-fetched as it initially sounds. The design world has recognized the likelihood and severity of both contingencies and unintended consequences. Recent work on concepts for universal design defines good design as that which minimizes the "hazards and the adverse consequences of accidental or unintended actions."[26] Good designers build "wiggle room" into products. That way, a product can be modified in the event it does not work as planned, the user employs it in some unanticipated way, or circumstances of use change dramatically. Ecologists have supported this idea of flexible design, maintaining that cars should be designed with fuel systems capable of running on a variety of fuels or admixtures thereof. No one knows what the economics of oil, gas, ethanol, etc. will be six years from now, because producers and consumers keep altering their behavior in response to new market signals and ideas.

Ethicists should follow the example of designers and ecologists and laud those individuals who try to incorporate flexibility into policies and rules. Given that some unintended consequences are very far afield from the original intent or quite removed in time from the initiating choices, planning for adaptability cannot prepare us for any and all unintended consequences. It would, though, be a respectful step in the right direction, a step toward developing an ethic of mindful preparedness.

*Intervene Cautiously, Ask Many Questions, and
Monitor Continually*

Whenever we adopt a new technique or practice, we should proceed cautiously, making only modest alterations in the system. The systems theorist Dietrich Dörner has shown that unintended consequences classically arise because we overlook crucial premises or because we respond to new data too aggressively. His studies of subjects' behavior suggest that we need another rule of thumb: *Any intervention to "improve" a situation should be done on a very modest scale.* Some effects are lagged. People who initiate large changes and who do not wait for lags to show themselves often overshoot the mark, inadvertently compounding an already bad situation. Dörner can be read as sketching some practical guidelines (not rules or laws) characteristic of the branch approach favored by Lindblom.

Continuing to gather information after devising an initial plan is key. Dörner discovered that the more thoughtful (and ultimately more effective) subjects asked many more "why" questions than less thoughtful actors. The subjects who inflicted the greatest harm were the ones who felt that their initial reflections and data gathering sufficed to give them an adequate understanding of the situation. (The Master of the Universe mentality rears its ugly head once again!) In Arendt's terms, the bad actors relied on pre-existing universals when judging the particular and did not use discussion to help them locate the universal within the unfolding particulars. These subjects ceased to evaluate the dynamic situation and stuck with the plan they had devised at the beginning of the period.[27] Even more chillingly, Dörner found that, when these individuals were given additional data, they hunkered down and committed more strongly to their original flawed plan. When subjects were informed that their development strategy was resulting in widespread famine, they responded, "Everyone has to die sometime"; "[The natives] will just have to pull in their belts and make sacrifices for the sake of their grandchildren"; and "It's mostly the old and weak who are dying, and that's good for the population structure." He concludes: "Helplessness generates cynicism," which leads to dangerous passivity and mindlessness.[28] One way to refine judgment and avoid becoming cynical is to proceed conservatively while monitoring the unfolding situation closely. To return to an earlier example: We ought not rest content with shipping donated mosquito nets to Africa. We need to follow up by finding out what the recipients actually have done with these nets.

Secure Relevant Expertise

Not even experts can anticipate completely unforeseeable adaptations to human actions, policies, and laws. This lack of omniscience, however, does not render expertise irrelevant. Some unintended consequences, while not anticipated in practice, are in principle predictable, especially if knowledgeable people share their insights with other concerned parties. Consider the subprime mortgage crisis, which came to a head in 2007–2008. This financial crisis involved obvious risks that were dismissed out of hand by major players in the real estate and derivatives markets. Taking huge risks had an enormous upside for many brokers and investors. Firms altered their behavior to capitalize on this upside after risk-restricting laws (e.g., Glass-Steagall Act of 1933) were repealed and deregulation implemented. While this widespread ratcheting up of leverage in response to shifts in risk-reward ratios was not meant to happen, it certainly could have been anticipated. In fact, Alan Greenspan, the former head of the Federal Reserve, has confessed that he believed that institutions' desire to preserve themselves would suffice to curtail what we now perceive was suicidal risk-taking. His statement is evidence that the increase in risk-taking that occurred was foreseeable by financial experts—members of the Federal Reserve considered precisely that possibility.

Moreover, regardless of what Greenspan and other bankers believed about the power and efficacy of corporate self-interest, corporate board members could have and should have inquired into the degree of risk firms were assuming and into the adequacy of measures to contain that risk. Risk management is a board duty. Yet some financial firms did not bother to secure directors with sufficient knowledge about leverage and expertise in financial services to ask appropriate questions or to grasp the full implications of what managers were telling the board. Bank of America's board has been roundly criticized for lacking meaningful financial experience.[29] Only three of Lehman's ten outside directors had any substantial background with financial institutions.[30] Although the other seven Lehman directors may have been clever and dedicated to doing a good job, their lack of experience made it unlikely that they would be able to evaluate intended, much less, unintended consequences.

Neither managerial nor directorial expertise is of much value if institutions make no routine effort to draw upon that knowledge. Knowledgeable discussions about risk need to become a regular part of institutional operations. After Tyco International Ltd. discovered that its CEO Dennis Koslowski and an associate had stolen around $600 million from the firm, it created, under the direction of its lead independent director, a rigorous risk-assessment process. Directors annually visit each of Tyco's business units and spend an entire day interviewing the units' managers and going over a checklist of possible risks and remedies.[31] This review directs agents' attention to dangers and downsides. In addition, these visits educate directors and other corporate leaders about the business of the firm on whose board they sit and the industry in which that firm operates. Greater background knowledge enables these leaders to think more clearly about risks.

Decide Court Cases Narrowly

Economists and sociologists have found ample examples of unintended consequences stemming from legislation. Law professor Cass Sunstein worries that court cases, too, create such outcomes. This concern has led him to advocate "judicial minimalism." Courts should focus "on the specific cases at hand and [avoid articulating] a position as

America's moral compass."[32] This more modest approach prevents the courts from rendering sweeping and perhaps hubristic judgments on highly contentious matters. Such judgments tend to compromise a court's moral authority. Judicial restraint, by contrast, keeps public policy issues within the political realm where these issues can be subjected to vigorous debate.[33] Public discussion can bring out hidden dimensions of extremely complex issues, helping us avoid adopting policies with unwelcome effects. By confining itself to the questions in the case before it, a court can more easily correct for any unintended consequences. Restraint is particularly desirable in light of the fast evolution of new technologies. Sunstein especially warns courts against pronouncing on how emerging technologies will affect and be affected by the First Amendment to the United States Constitution: "Even though the First Amendment is first, it would be best for the court to be humble and cautious rather than set out some rules that might be bad or confounded by new circumstances and technologies."[34]

This minimalist approach is not without difficulty. When court rulings are very narrow, the other branches of government are unable to garner or extrapolate principles for guiding subsequent behavior. A series of narrow rulings on a similar topic (e.g., holding detainees as part of the war on terror) may send mixed signals. That lack of clarity may itself produce unintended consequences. Nevertheless, on balance, it may well be better for courts to decide cases narrowly in order to maintain maximal flexibility for heading off and dealing with perverse effects.

Psychological Remedies

Chapter 2 showed how relying upon past cases either too little or too much produces unintended consequences. This observation suggests the following psychological rules of thumb.

Consider past cases so as to apply existing theories more mindfully

When we are dealing with regularly occurring effects for which we have a large number of data points, standard utilitarian, deontological, care, and virtue moralities can help us arrive at good, or at least defensible, positions. These theories offer insight when outcomes are foreseeable. And the more frequent the purposive behavior in question and the clearer the link between cause and effect, the more foreseeable the likely consequences of that behavior become. We should not, therefore, completely ignore the past when planning our choices. Instead, we should test what we know from history, asking ourselves in what respect present and past cases are similar and where they diverge.

It seems likely, for example, that the subprime mortgage crisis will prompt the Federal Reserve Bank to enforce capital requirements on any remaining broker firms similar to those requirements imposed upon commercial banks after the 1980s savings and loan debacle. On the face of it, such a requirement appears prudent. During the credit boom, brokers borrowed heavily. At present, brokers' leverage is often double or triple the level seen at commercial banks.[35]

If broker-dealers are going to have the benefit of a governmental safety net, then the central bank may reasonably ask these parties to become less leveraged. But caution is advisable. Firms subject to stiffer requirements will have either to issue more equity or sell assets to pay down debt in order to meet stricter capital requirements. Either response almost certainly will depress broker firms' stocks, making their leverage ratios even worse, thereby compounding the crisis. To avoid biting that particular bullet, firms may be tempted to take their most toxic assets off balance sheet. Such a shifting of bad assets is exactly the move made by commercial banks and S&Ls in the 1980s and 1990s. The resulting loss of financial transparency played into the current financial crisis, which is a lesson we should keep in mind if the Federal Reserve tightens capital requirements on various financial institutions. Already bankers are cleverly adapting and playing games when calculating their leverage ratios, treating some debt as non-debt in an effort to make their firms appear less leveraged than they really are.[36] Recalling our experiences from the S&L crisis, we should be on the lookout for these sorts of shenanigans.

Fuel economy standards offer a good example of how we can learn from the unintended consequences of the past. As I noted in Chapter 1, the tightening of automobile fuel economy standards under CAFE did not reduce emissions as much as regulators had hoped. Efficiency-compliant cars cost more, so people held on to dirty gas guzzlers longer than they might have if car manufacturers had not been legislatively required to produce more fuel efficient cars.[37] In addition, emissions actually went up to some extent, because greater efficiency meant that people could drive further and more often for the same cost of fuel. There was a third reason why CAFE was not as effective as had been hoped: The auto industry responded to the new law by producing and then heavily promoting trucks and SUVs. These vehicles were not subject to the tough fuel economy standards applicable to cars. They got substantially worse gas mileage and were dirtier than sedans and smaller vehicles.

The gradual realization of these untoward, offsetting consequences led scholars to study the various effects of more stringent fuel economy standards on emissions. Their data are now available to help us think more critically about the new national fuel economy standards proposed by President Obama in 2009. The standards will supposedly make cars cleaner and lessen global warming while at the same time reducing US dependence on foreign oil. The past teaches us that we ought to see the downsides as well as upsides to pollution-related legislation. It is a good sign that the public debate in America about regulations has been more nuanced this time around. On the one hand, the Clean Air Act's standards did lower emissions of carbon monoxide (down 52% since 1980), ozone (down 41%), and nitrogen dioxide (down 37%). Almost everyone accepts that high levels of pollution impose serious human and economic costs (e.g., chronic bronchitis, premature death, asthma, lost days of work, etc.). On the other hand, we now realize stricter fuel economy standards will likely produce a spike in traffic deaths because new compliant vehicles will weigh less. The National Resource Center, after reviewing the effects of the earlier CAFE legislation, concluded that the downsizing of vehicles since 1980 "while resulting in significant fuel savings, . . . [also] resulted in a safety penalty" of up to 2,600 more vehicle crash deaths than would have occurred without the legislation.[38] We have learned as well that forecasts of emission reductions to be gained by tightening fuel economy standards must incorporate the so-called "rebound effect"—the increase in driving that occurs when drivers of more fuel-efficient cars realize that they can drive more since they are saving on fuel costs.

The Obama administration has prudently incorporated this rebound effect into projected fuel savings. What needs further consideration is the deferred purchase effect. If car prices go up (as they almost certainly will with the new legislation—the Obama administration expects the average price of a car to increase by $1300 by 2016 because of the new fuel economy standards) many poorer customers will keep their clunkers. Today we understand that most pollution can be traced back to the oldest cars on the roads. Recent research has established that 50% of smog and carbon monoxide comes from the dirtiest 10% of cars. Even more striking, 80% of pollution is produced by the dirtiest 30% of cars.[39] If we are not mindful, we will wind up increasing, rather than reducing, emissions. The so-called "cash for clunkers" bill has given consumers a hefty incentive of up to $4500 to buy a new "advanced technology car." However, people who are able to afford a brand new car do not need any incentive to underwrite their purchase. It is the working class and lower middle class that could really use the cash back. Historical data suggests that Congress should consider providing incentives for purchases of used cars. The environment benefits when someone trades up from a 1987 Oldsmobile to a used 2004 Toyota. Some states (e.g., Texas[40]) have successfully experimented with extending cash for clunkers legislation to used car purchases. We ought to obtain and use such local data when preparing national legislation.

My larger point is that we can learn from history about past unintended consequences and then use that knowledge to make better policy the next time around. In those cases where the past closely resembles the present, judicious use of well-vetted data will better ground moral judgments arrived at using utilitarian, Kantian, care, and virtue moralities.

Make analysis more dynamic by incorporating empirical findings regarding foreseeable unintended consequences

We should not, though, uncritically rely upon similar past cases. Analogies are not identities. This caveat suggests another rule of thumb: Gather empirical data before rushing to judgment. Ethical thinking needs to move beyond mere abstraction to incorporate ongoing empirical research as an integral part of analysis. Philosophers, theologians, and other moralists should shed the notion moral thinking consists in applying standard rules to situations, rendering a judgment, and then moving on to the next case or dilemma. Real ethical thinking requires looking at empirical findings over time, revisiting issues repeatedly.

Take the following question: Would it be right to introduce a so-called "living wage" into the City of New Orleans? When such an ordinance was proposed in 2002, many worried that it would lead to lay-offs of lower-wage workers. Small businesses would not, opponents argued, be able to afford the wage increase and might relocate out of New Orleans in order to avoid having to pay it. The intent to help the poor was laudable, but might not the legislation produce predictable but unintended consequences resulting in more harm than good?

This question cannot be answered properly in the abstract. We need both data and a sophisticated model incorporating factors such as the elasticity of demand and supply curves and the speed with which a living wage ordinance might be introduced. The desirability of a living wage turns out to be a highly nuanced issue, as several authors found when they performed a detailed empirical analysis in 2002:

> Our results suggest that the New Orleans firms would have been able to absorb most, if not all, the increased costs of the proposed living wage ordinance through some combination of price and productivity increases or redistribution within the firm. This result flows most basically from the main finding of our survey research: that living wage cost increases will amount to about 0.9 percent of operating budgets for average firms in New Orleans and no more than 2.2 percent of operating budgets for the city's restaurant industry, which is the industry with the highest average cost increase. This then also suggests that the incentive for covered firms to lay

off low-wage employees or relocate outside the New Orleans city limits should be correspondingly weak. It would have been likely, however, that some displacement of the least well-credentialed workers would occur as a result of the ordinance, though again, this effect should also be relatively modest. Similarly, a relatively small number of New Orleans firms likely would have relocated, generating a loss of municipal tax revenues on the order of 0.5 percent of the city's budget. Generally, though, the process through which New Orleans firms would have adjusted the living wage ordinance likely would have been relatively mild, as the overall $71 million burden in increased wages and payroll taxes would have been broadly diffused among the city's 12,700 firms as well as the city government.[41]

After Hurricane Katrina, this analysis would have to be redone, and the results might well be quite different. Perhaps the New Orleans economy after the flooding is simply too fragile to cope with an imposed living wage. Ethical analysis must be dynamic, mining new data and honing empirical models in an effort to capture and evaluate unintended yet foreseeable consequences.

The requisite data should be gathered over months, if not years. Human beings are prone to believe the hype about the latest technique. These fads, though, play themselves out in unexpected ways. A long-term perspective and time series data are needed. As is well-known, the Japanese pioneered "just-in-time" (JIT) manufacturing. JIT delivers inventory to the factory only when it is needed, enabling firms to reduce inventory carrying costs. The idea was well-executed by Japanese manufacturers, so Detroit auto companies and other American and European manufacturers rushed to adopt JIT. Lost in this stampede were some relevant facts. As JIT became more popular in Japan, a major problem emerged. JIT worked only if trucks arrived at factories on time. With more firms adopting JIT, Japanese city streets became clogged with trucks trying to make deliveries. Traffic jam costs started to exceed the warehouse costs, and the air quality in cities suffered as hundreds of trucks idled their engines. Adaptive limitations such as this one take time to become apparent. It is important, therefore, not to become uncritically enamored with the latest fashion or fad. We should expect that the latest and greatest will turn out to be only partially a good thing. Foreseen benefits will be offset by some unanticipated costs at both the organizational and social level.

Pay Close Attention to Possible Effects of Alterations in Costs and Incentives

Chapter 1 cited examples of unintended consequences arising when changes were made to incentives or to any factors impacting the bottom line of individuals or corporations. We need to be especially careful when we alter rewards and costs or the way in which we account for such things. When a firm's costs increase, it typically responds by finding ways to slash those costs or to avoid incurring them in the first place. When a new financial instrument comes onto the market, traders and investment bankers characteristically seek to use it in any way possible to make money. Changes in laws and rules inevitably produce loopholes and invite creative and possibly deviant responses. In the 1980s,

> Congress, intent on "rescuing" the S&L industry in the face of virtually insuperable market forces, suspended GAAP (Generally Accepted Accounting Principles) reporting and continued to guarantee deposits with taxpayer funds. This created an environment that fostered everything from aggressive overinvestment in high-risk commercial real estate all the way to basic fraud. Estimates of the eventual cleanup under the 1989 Financial Institutions Reform, Recovery, and Enforcement Act (FIRREA) range from $500 billion to $1 trillion, taking into account direct payments made by the FDIC, the lost equity of S&L investors, and administrative and other costs.[42]

It was readily foreseeable that the suspension of GAAP would attract cheats and lead to fraud. People would think that they could get away with doing just about anything to make money. That is precisely what occurred. Business ethicists should criticize not only these shysters but also the complete lack of prudence on the part of senators and representatives who drafted this irresponsible legislation with no regard to how they were affecting costs and incentives.

Watch Out for Common, Well-Documented Biases

Some unintended consequences can nevertheless be foreseen if we attend to well-documented psychological biases. In 2000, Sweden introduced a partially privatized market-based social retirement system. The government sent all adult Swedish citizens a personalized letter explaining that they could invest up to 2.5% of their annual pay in new portfolio funds run by private firms. The remaining 18.5% of saved annual income would continue to flow into the traditional government pension system. Swedes were told that they could invest that 2.5% in a default, low-cost index style fund or place it with any of the other 456 approved funds. Only one-third of the Swedes chose the safer default fund; around 65% opted to put money with smaller private pension firms. Richard Thaler and Henrik Cronqvist, two behavioral economists, found that these less diversified funds fared far worse over a three-year period than the default fund. Investors were led astray by two types of known biases. Many Swedes fell prey to an "extrapolation bias." Seduced by high-flying tech funds' recent returns, they wrongly assumed that the returns would continue to be good and so failed to diversify adequately. (By contrast, the default fund was well-diversified.) Another group succumbed to the well-known "familiarity bias." Being Swedish, these investors felt more comfortable with Swedish stocks and put a disproportionately large portion of their monies into these stocks.[43] Once again they failed to diversify as much as would have been prudent.

These findings accord with the research of the psychologists Amos Tversky and Daniel Kahneman. They found that, contrary to what classical economists assume, human beings do not start with a fixed set of preferences. When faced with uncertainty, we fall back on rules of thumb and create our preferences on the fly.[44] In other words, we are not completely rational beings who optimize our well-being with every choice. Instead, we are frail organisms who do the best we can while frequently succumbing to various sorts of unacknowledged psychological biases or prejudices.

If so, when we propose changes to the status quo, we should consider which types of biases are likely to come into play as people adapt to those changes. If the United States were to privatize some part of Social Security, senators and representatives should admit upfront that not every citizen will invest rationally and wisely. Unscrupulous marketers will try to capitalize on extrapolation or familiarity biases. The Swedish experience suggests that, when advertising for fund choices is very heavy (as it likely would be giving the billions of dollars in American retirement funds at stake), many people will think it in their best interest to construct their own stock portfolios. Average citizens may not grasp the importance of spreading risk through diversification. American policy-makers, therefore, might consider offering fewer choices and ensuring that these choices promote adequate diversification. At a minimum, should politicians decide to tinker with the retirement system, they ought to admit explicitly the existence of such biases and take steps to ameliorate untoward effects, lest efforts to save the social security system wind up imperiling it.

Seek to Become Aware of Individual Prejudices

We all have biases. The trick is to become aware of them. Researchers at Harvard have devised a way to test for prejudices of which we are not conscious or which we do not wish to admit. The Implicit Association Test probes whether subjects have an easier time associating some words (e.g., positive words) with one group (e.g., whites) than with another (e.g., African-Americans). The test measures physical response times and error rates when subjects are asked to pair words with carefully chosen images. The test has been used in social and clinical psychology and has been extensively vetted. The IAT suggests that some of the cognitive processes coloring our perceptions and interpretations of past and present events are unconscious. Using the test and other such instruments to become more cognizant of our possible biases may enable us to check, or at least reduce, the effects of prejudice. Such reduction is desirable, for our biases can keep us from hearing what others have to say. If we are unable to tap into these perspectives, we cannot draw upon others' experiences to help us better foretell possible bad effects of well-meaning deeds and policies.

There is another reason for becoming aware of personal biases. When we are oblivious to how others are viewing our actions, we may act in a way that others interpret very differently than we intend. Social scientists recognize this possibility by distinguishing a person's agency from his or her desires. Agency describes "the subject's capacity to make meanings in her interaction with others."[45] These meanings may not be planned or intended at a conscious or even subliminal level. They may simply result from an agent's ignorance of how others are reading a gesture or interpreting a phrase. What one person considers insignificant or meaningless may be fraught with symbolism for another party. Desire, by contrast, refers to the want or felt need that drives or compels action. Although we may not desire or intend a certain effect, we may bring it about through our agency. When we are more self-aware of our prejudices and blindspots, we can align desire and agency, thereby minimizing this source of unintended consequences.

Be Skeptical of Prophecies

Politicians and policy-makers frequently make doomsday pronouncements. These prophecies should be taken with a psychological grain, if not a boulder, of salt. When citizens hear these warnings, they often adapt their behavior in such a way that the dire outcomes do not occur. Warnings about unabated populate growth giving rise to mass starvation caused countries to promote birth control and spurred scientists to invent more productive crops. Starvation still looms in many nations, but mass deaths are not, contrary to what some politicians prophesied, an inevitable consequence of population growth.

Predictions that commodity prices would soar due to scarce natural resources are another case in point. Whenever suppliers see a possibility to make profits by providing substitutes for scarce commodities, they move in and provide competing goods. This substitution effect has kept commodity prices steady or, in some cases, even lowered them.[46] The economist Julian Simon and population theorist Paul Ehrlich (author of *The Population Bomb*) made a famous wager in 1980. Ehrlich thought that commodity prices would necessarily rise because of increasing populations and soaring demand. Simon countered that commodity prices were just as likely to go down. People would discover how to produce and substitute other goods if prices were to rise. Simon said he would bet a thousand dollars that prices of five raw, non-regulated commodities (to be chosen by Ehrlich) would not rise in the long run (defined as a decade). Ehrlich picked five commodities, and then each man bought $200 worth of paper versions of these five using prices as of September 29, 1980, for a total bet of $1000. On September 29, 1990, they re-priced this basket of commodities.

> Between 1980 and 1990, the world's population grew by more than 800 million. . . . But by September 1990, without a single exception, the price of each of Ehrlich's selected metals had fallen. . . . Chrome, which had sold for $3.90 a pound in 1980, was down to $3.70 in 1990. Tin, which was $8.72 a pound in 1980, was down to $3.88 a decade later.[47]

The next month Ehrlich wrote a check to Simon for around $600 to settle the bet.

Such adaptability means that, although Hans Jonas is right to emphasize our ability to damage the earth in possibly irreparable ways, we need to think twice before concluding that the sky is about to fall.

All of [Ehrlich's] grim predictions [were] decisively over-turned by events. Ehrlich was wrong about higher natural resource prices, about "famines of unbelievable proportions" occurring by 1975, about "hundreds of millions of people starving to death" in the 1970s and '80s, about the world "entering a genuine age of scarcity." In 1990, for his having promoted "greater public understanding of environ-mental problems," Ehrlich received a MacArthur Founda-tion Genius Award. [Simon] always found it somewhat peculiar that . . . neither . . . his public wager with Ehrlich nor anything else that [Simon] did, said, or wrote seemed to make much of a dent on the world at large. For some reason he could never comprehend, people were inclined to believe the very worst about anything and everything; they were immune to contrary evidence just as if they'd been medically vaccinated against the force of fact. Furthermore, there seemed to be a bizarre reverse-Cassandra effect operating in the universe: Whereas the mythical Cassandra spoke the awful truth and was not believed, these days "experts" spoke awful falsehoods, and they were believed.[48]

Whenever we hear someone warn of horrific consequences resulting from some trend, we should not panic but rather observe how, upon hearing this forecast, people start to alter their behavior and to create alternatives. By casting our eye in that direction, we may be able to anticipate unintended consequences that are the polar opposite of what the doomsayers are foretelling. In addition, training ourselves to be skeptical will help tame our animal spirits. As we become less reactive, we will judge more objectively.

Cultivate Prévoyance

The great French general Champlain was aware of the unpredictability of human affairs and advocated the conscious cultivation of a *prévoyant* attitude.[49] There is no exact English equivalent for this French word. It literally means "seeing before," but translating the word as "foresight" does not capture its full meaning. David Fischer has described it as "the power of a prepared mind to act upon chance events in a world of deep uncertainty."[50] Champlain did not possess the gift of prophecy, but he did seek to prepare himself for surprise events. He began by accepting that we live in a world of contingencies and unintended consequences. Champlain knew early on his life that we do not have the power to manipulate and control everything that happens to us. His second step was to treat other people kindly. By respecting the native tribes in Canada and by learning their languages, Champlain benefited from their goodwill. Before he began trading with them, he attended one of their large gatherings and spent days partying with them and building rapport. As a result of the interest and goodwill he showed the various tribes, they shared information with him. The knowledge he gained enabled him to avoid or to recover from serious mistakes. To this day the native tribes of Canada remember Champlain as a great man and leader.

People who demonstrate goodwill toward each other are better able to work together to cope with any unintended consequences that do arise. Crises can then serve as opportunities for, rather than as obstacles to, mutual development and prosperity. *Prévoyance* is helpful in another way. The term refers to the practice of "learning to make sound judgments on the basis of imperfect knowledge. Mainly it is about taking a broad view in projects of large purpose and about thinking for the long run."[51] Individuals concerned only with short-term gains, by definition, are not considering the likelihood of unintended consequences emerging months, or even years, hence. By contrast, those who seek to understand the meaning of an action in its fullest context and who try to develop a larger systems view of how things and events are enmeshed with each other (which is not the same as looking for universal laws but more akin to an ecological perspective) develop a prepared mind equipped to deal well with surprises.

Defer Judgment in the Present in Order to Judge Better in the Future

Even if we adopt the psychological remedies discussed above, the bitter truth remains that many events and actions produce unforeseeable consequences. Not all effects are regular. We do not always have many data points. Gathering time series data may prove difficult or even impossible. How people respond and adapt to an event or to a change in laws or incentives will depend upon many subtle factors. Given that we are never going to be able to foresee all possible unintended consequences, we might find it useful to adopt an attitude or psychological stance rooted in Chinese Daoist thinking.

The following short Chinese tale nicely illustrates this altitude:

Once upon a time, there was a king. The king liked one of his subjects very much, for this man was wise and consistently gave useful advice. The king took him along wherever he went. While the two men were out hunting, the king was bitten by a dog. His injured finger became infected. The king asked his advisor if the infection was a bad sign. The advisor replied, "Good or bad, hard to say." In the end, the finger of the king had to be amputated. The king again asked the follower if the dog's bite was a bad thing. The follower gave the same answer: "Good or bad, hard to say." Enraged by this apparently cavalier and unsympathetic response, the king imprisoned his advisor. Time passed. The king continued to hunt. One day he got excited as he chased a huge buck. Penetrating ever deeper into the thicket of trees, he soon found himself lost. To make matters worse, he was captured by natives living deep within this jungle. They prepared to sacrifice him to their god. But when they noticed that the king had one finger missing, they released him immediately. He was not perfect and thus not suitable for sacrifice.

The king managed to get back to his palace. The king thought that he finally understood his advisor's expression, "Good or bad, hard to say." If he had not lost his finger, he would have been killed by the native people. The king ordered his advisor released and apologized to him. To the king's amazement, the man was not in the least bit angry. Instead, he calmly said, "There is no need for you to apologize. It wasn't necessarily a bad thing that you locked me up. If you hadn't jailed me, you would have taken me with you into the jungle. Upon finding that you were not suitable, the natives would have sacrificed me instead!"

This scenario might be thought to involve only historical contingencies, not unintended consequences. The king makes no adaptive response either after he is injured or after he consigns the advisor to jail. He simply reacts to what he takes to be a series of undesirable events (being bitten by a dog, captured by the natives). Closer consideration reveals an adaptive response—on the part of the advisor. *Having learned that the world works in mysterious ways and gives rise to both contingent and unintended consequences, the king's advisor has consciously embraced a strategy of deferring judgment.* The advisor does not endorse moral relativism. He never denies that some acts are beneficial, others harmful. What he does maintain is that rendering sound judgments is extremely difficult in a dynamic world rife with uncertainty. He mindfully assumes a more neutral stance, refusing to react emotionally first to this event and then to that one. This practiced stance reins in his animal spirits.

From this Daoist perspective, ethical analysis consists neither in applying norms to a situation nor in building large elaborate systems. Practical wisdom consists rather in consciously deferring judgment now in order to render better judgments later. Prudent people monitor the results of decisions and avoid getting caught up in fear, hype, or dire prophesies. Through dispassionate scrutiny, they distill what experience has taught them and become ever more skilled at discerning regularities. The practically wise learn that altering incentives and cost structures generally leads corporations and individuals to adapt their behaviors in somewhat predictable ways. They then use this insight when it comes time to assess the desirability of a proposed plan to lower or raise incentives or costs. In those cases where the past offers little help in predicting outcomes, they imitate the king's advisor—they acknowledge their lack of omniscience, gently caution others to tread carefully, argue for smaller changes instead of radical or grand gestures, and then patiently watch as events unfold.

CONCLUSION

These suggested remedies should be taken as tentative proposals designed to jumpstart a conversation about how to act ethically in a world of unintended consequences. This conversation requires us to move away from our habitual ways of thinking about morality. Nigel Dower correctly cautions:

> It is all too easy to think that what morality really requires of us is to avoid intentionally doing harm to one another, to avoid deceiving, stealing, letting down, assaulting, libeling one another, and so on, and that, in general, what really counts in moral assessment is what one aims at or intends . . . That might all be very well if we lived in a world where the unintended consequences of our actions did not materially affect the conditions under which others pursued their objectives. . . . But the world is not like this. . . .[1]

It is high time that applied ethicists, social scientists, organizational theorists, policy-makers, and politicians admit the existence and pervasiveness of this live dragon of

145

unintended consequences and incorporate them into our choices, judgments, worldview, and practices. We cannot slay this dragon. So it is best that we adopt Tolkien's advice and start trying to live with it as mindfully as possible.

Notes

Introduction

1.   Jon Elster, *Logic and Society, Contradictions and Possible Worlds* (London: Wiley, 1978); Raymond Boudon, *The Logic of Social Action* (London: Routledge & Kegan Paul, 1981); Robert K. Merton, "The Unintended Consequences of Purposive Social Action," *American Sociological Review* 1, no. 6 (December, 1936): 894–904. These authors focus primarily on the nature of intentional action, the various causes of unintended consequences, and the viability of the analytical concept "unintended consequence" or "perverse effect" in accounts of social change.

2.   J. R. R. Tolkien, *The Hobbit* (Boston, MA: Houghton Mifflin Company, 1994), 294.

Chapter 1

1. Tarina Kleyn and Jürgens Jozefowicz, "Wasteland Created by Human Hands," *Hamburg Evening News*, 28 and 29 December 1985.

2. Carol Peasley, "Is Aid Really 'Dead'?" *Huffington Post*, http://www.huffingtonpost.com/carol-peasley/is-aid-really-dead_b_189613.html; accessed 21 April 2009.

3. Dambisa Moyo, "Why Foreign Aid Is Hurting Africa," *Wall Street Journal*, 21 March 2009; http://online.wsj.com/article/SB123758895999200083.html; accessed 23 March 2009.

4. Ibid.

5. Associated Press, "Cigarette Design May Boost Risks," *Wall Street Journal*, 19 May 2009; http://online.wsj.com/article/SB124270030097533303.html; accessed 19 May 2009.

6. The Scotsman James Dunbar quoted in Christopher J. Berry, *Social Theory of the Scottish Enlightenment* (Edinburgh: Edinburgh University Press, 1997), 45.

7. Geoff Fernie, "Report on Rehabilitation Research: The Power of Research," Toronto Rehabilitation Laboratory, available from torontorehab.com/research/documents/TR6report.pdf; accessed 19 May 2009.

8. John Wodatch, "ADA Audio Conference," 18 May 2004; http://www.ada-audio.org/Archives/?type=transcript&id=2004–05–18; accessed 8 February 2008.

9. George Herbert, *Jacula Prudentum* (London: T.M. for T. Garthwait 1651), Proverb #499.

10. Thomas DeLeire, "The Unintended Consequences of the Americans with Disabilities Act," *Regulation* 23, no. 1 (2000): 21–24.

11. Dean Lueck and Jeffrey Michael, "Preemptive Habitat Destruction under the Endangered Species Act," *The Journal of Law and Economics* 46 (2003): 27–60. See also Daowei Zhang, "Endangered Species and Timber Harvesting: The Case of Red-Cockaded Woodpeckers," *Economic Inquiry* 42, no. 1 (2004): 150–165.

12. Hubert H. Humphrey quoted in *Newsweek*, 23 January 1978, p. 23.

13. Sandra C. Vera-Munoz, "Corporate Governance Reforms: Redefined Expectations of Audit Committee Responsibilities and Effectiveness," *Journal of Business Ethics* 62, no. 2 (December 2005): 115–127.

14. Julie H. Daum and Thomas J. Neff, "The Numbers Are In . . . and Soundly Rising," *Directors & Boards* (Fall, 2003): 23. Neff predicted the dramatic rise in director compensation at a conference in early 2002.

15. Ibid.

16. *Wall Street Journal*, "Millionaires Go Missing," 27 May 2009; http://online.wsj.com/article/SB124329282377252471.html; accessed 28 May 2009.

17. Ibid.

18. Arthur Laffer and Stephen Moore, "Soak the Rich, Lose the Rich," *Wall Street Journal*, 18 May 2009; http://online.wsj.com/article/SB124260067214828295.html; accessed 18 May 2009.

19. Ibid.

20. Feldstein's and Poulson's studies cited in Laffer and Moore, "Soak the Rich."

21. See table of standards in NHTSA, "Automotive Fuel Economy Program: Annual Update Calendar Year 2003," http://www.nhtsa.dot.gov/cars/rules/cafe/FuelEconUpdates/2003/index.htm; accessed 8 January 2006.

22. Andrew Grieve and Steve Dickinson, "China's New Labor Law"; http://www.chinalawblog.com/2008/05/chinas_new_labor_contract_law_1.html; accessed 10 April 2007.

23. Shu-Ching Jean Chen, "Mass Layoffs? In Booming China?" *Forbes*, 13 November 2007; http://www.forbes.com/2007/11/13/china-mass-layoffs-markets-econ-cx_jc_1113markets02.html; accessed 14 November 2007.

24. Catherine M. Sharkey, "Unintended Consequences of Medical Malpractice Damages Caps," *NYU Law Review* 80 (2005): 391–512.

25. Treasury department quoted in Jason Zweig, "Pay Collars Won't Hold Back Wall Street's Big Dogs," *Wall Street Journal*, 7 February 2009, p. B1.

26. Mark Maremont and Joann S. Lublin, "Loopholes Sap Potency of Pay," *Wall Street Journal*, 6 February 2009, p. C1.

27. The Obama administration eventually abandoned the proposed caps.

28. The possibility that compensating directors with stock or stock options might create a moral hazard was foreseen by a few people. See, e.g., James Kristie, "A Delicious Irony in Governance Ideology," *Directors & Boards* (Summer, 1999) in which he asks: "Why does stock ownership by directors enhance their independence, but stock ownership by auditors makes them less independent? What is the board but an 'auditor' of management?"

29. Danielle Lee, "Mattel Recalls More China-Manufactured Toys," *CRO Newsletter*; http://www.thecro.com/node/521; accessed 5 September 2007.

30. "Vermont Journal; Billboard Ban? Try a 19-Foot Genie!" *New York Times*, 16 January 1991; http://www.nytimes.com/1991/01/16/us/vermont-journal-billboard-ban-try-a-19-foot-genie.html; accessed 10 July 2007.

31. Jared D. Harris and Philip Bromiley, "Incentives to Cheat: The Influence of Executive Compensation and Firm Performance on Financial Misrepresentation," *Organization Science* 18, no. 3 (2006): 350–367.

Chapter 2

1. Gavin Kennedy, "Adam Smith's Invisible Hand: From Metaphor to Myth." Paper presented at the 34th Annual Meeting of the History of Economics Society, George Mason University, Fairfax, Virginia, June 10, 2007.

2. Ricardo Hausman quoted in Andrew Ross Sorkin, ed., "The Big Imbalance in the Room," blog entry from the Davos Conference, *New York Times*; http://dealbook.blogs.nytimes.com/category/davos-2009/; accessed 28 January 2009.

3. William A. Cohen, *A Class with Drucker: The Lost Lessons of the World's Greatest Management Teacher* (New York: AMACON, 2007), 163.

4. Richard Wolin, *Heidegger's Children: Hannah Arendt, Karl Lowith, Hans Jonas, and Herbert Marcuse* (Princeton, NJ: Princeton University Press, 2001), 111.

5. Hans Jonas, *The Phenomenon of Life: Toward a Philosophical Biology* (Evanston, IL: Northwestern University Press, 2001), 3.

6. Wolin, *Heidegger's Children*, 115.

7. Ibid., 117–118.

8. For further discussion of this human gap, see Peter Senge, *The Fifth Discipline: The Art and Practice of the Learning Organization* (New York: Random House Business Books, 1993); James Botkin, Mahdi Elmandjra and Mircea Malita, *No Limits to Learning: Bridging the Human Gap* (Oxford: Pergamon Press, 1979).

9. Robert E. Ulanowicz, "Life after Newton: An Ecological Metaphysic," *BioSystems* 50, no. 2 (1999): 127–142. In discussing these five characteristics, I have drawn extensively upon Ulanowicz's wonderful article.

10. Ibid., 135.

11. Ibid., 138–139.

12. Translation mine. I based my translation on the Greek text published in Herodotus, *History*, trans. A.D. Godley (Cambridge, MA: Harvard University Press, 1975), book 1, secs. 1–5.

13. Ibid., sec. 5.

14. Ibid., sec. 6.

15. Ibid., sec. 5.

16. William McKinley and Andreas G. Scherer, "Some Unanticipated Consequences of Organizational Restructuring," *Academy of Management Review* 25 (2000): 735–753.

17. Ibid., 740.

18. Guowei Jian, "Unpacking Unintended Consequences in Organizational Change: A Process Model," *Management Communication Quarterly* 21, no. 1 (2007): 5–28.

19. Ibid., 14.

20. Ludwig von Mises, *Human Action: A Treatise on Economics* (Indianapolis, IN: Liberty Fund, 2007), 1: 105–106.

21. Ibid., 1: 113.
22. Forster quoted in Zadie Smith, "E.M. Forster, Middle Manager: The BBC Talks of E.M. Forster, 1929–1969," *New York Review of Books* 55, no. 13 (14 August 2008); http://www.nybooks.com/articles/21692; accessed on 5 December 2008.
23. Robert K. Merton, *On Social Structure and Science* (Chicago, IL: University of Chicago Press, 1996), 178.
24. George A. Akerlof and Robert J. Shiller, *Animal Spirits: How Human Psychology Drives the Economy and Why It Matters for Global Capitalism* (Princeton, NJ: Princeton University Press, 2009), passim.
25. Jill Bolte Taylor, *My Stroke of Insight* (Detroit, MI: Thorndike Press, 2006), large print edition, 37.
26. Jean-Jacques Rousseau quoted in Paul A. Rahe, *Soft Despotism* (New Haven, CT: Yale University Press, 2009), 119.
27. Robert Lee Hotz, "Testosterone May Fuel Stock-Market Success, Or Make Traders Tipsy," *Wall Street Journal*, 18 April 2008, p. B1.
28. *Science Daily*, "Testosterone Levels Predict City Traders' Profitability," 15 April 2008; http://www.sciencedaily.com/releases/2008/04/080414174855.htm; accessed 17 April 2008.
29. Charles Handy, *The Age of Paradox* (Boston, MA: Harvard Business School Press, 1994), 12.
30. Craig R. Fox and Amos Tversky, "A Belief-Based Account of Decision-Making under Uncertainty," *Management Science* 44, no. 7: 879–895.
31. Petter Johansson, Lars Hall, and S. Sikstrom, "From Change Blindness to Choice Blindness," *Psychologia* 51, no. 2 (2008): 142–155.
32. For a good discussion of how the framing of issues leads agents to embrace false conclusions, see Raymond Boudon, *The Art of Self-Persuasion* (Malden, MA: Blackwell Publishers Inc., 1994).
33. D.J. Simons and C.F. Chabris, "Gorillas in Our Midst: Sustained Inattentional Blindness for Dynamic Events," *Perception* 28, no. 9 (1999): 1059–1074.

34. Dolly Chugh and Max H. Bazerman, "Bounded Awareness: What You Fail to See Can Hurt You," *Mind & Society* 6 (2007): 3.

35. Robert K. Merton, "The Unintended Consequences of Purposive Social Action," *American Sociological Review* 1, no. 6 (December, 1936): 894–904.

36. James A. Kaplan, "The Perverse Effect of Credit Default Swaps: A Catastrophe in the Making," Chairman's Corner, *Audit Integrity*, 17 June 2008; http://auditintegrity.com; accessed 17 June 2008.

37. Pierre Coste, the French translator of John Locke, quoted in Rahe, *Soft Despotism*, 41.

38. John Locke, *An Essay Concerning Human Understanding*, bk. 2, ch. 21, sec. 56; http://arts.cuhk.edu.hk/Philosophy/Locke/echu/ed; accessed 13 June 2008.

39. Tocqueville quoted in Rahe, *Soft Despotism*, 179.

40. Charles Giancarlo, "The Internet Accelerates While U.S. Trails Behind," *San Francisco Chronicle*, 14 December 2006, p. B7.

41. D. W. Berkus, "Ten Trends in Technology;" http://www.slideshare.net/guest223e63/ten-dominant-trends-in-technology-2008-fall-2008-version-presentation; accessed 10 December 2008.

42. Ibid.

Chapter 3

1. John Stuart Mill, *Utilitarianism* (New York: Dover Publications, 2007), especially chapter 1.

2. Immanuel Kant, *Groundwork of the Metaphysics of Morals*, trans. H.J. Paton (New York: Harper Perennial, 1964), passim.

3. Ibid., 89.

4. Ibid., 72.

5. Carol Gilligan, *In a Different Voice* (Cambridge, MA: Harvard University Press, 1982), 100, 159–60.

6. Bernard Yack, "Injustice and the Victim's Voice," *Michigan Law Review* 89 (1991): 1334, 1342–1343.

7. For an account that does sketch necessary conditions for dialogue that is both caring and just, see Daryl Koehn, *Rethinking Feminist Ethics* (London: Routledge, 1998).
8. Aristotle, *Nicomachean Ethics*, trans. W.D. Ross, bk. 3, sec. 1.
9. Hans Jonas, *The Phenomenon of Life: Toward a Philosophical Biology* (Evanston, IL: Northwestern University Press, 2001), 117–118.
10. Ibid.
11. Ibid.

Chapter 4

1. Elsewhere I have distinguished between an ethic and a morality. Put simply, an ethic is rooted in greater self-awareness. It views evil as suffering arising from a false sense of self. Morality, by contrast, treats the communal welfare as primary, and construes evil as a violation of norms often stemming from poorly formed or malicious intentions. For a more sustained discussion of the distinction, see Daryl Koehn, *The Nature of Evil* (New York: Palgrave MacMillan, 2005), passim. In this chapter, my focus is on ethics, for I wish to consider what kind of practices, attitudes and worldviews increase awareness of the self and the self's effects on the world and on other people.
2. Cornelia Dean, "As Glaciers Melt, It's the Land That's Rising," *New York Times* online edition, 17 May, 2009.
3. Charles E. Lindblom, "The Science of 'Muddling Through'," *Public Administration Review* 19 (Spring, 1959): 79–88.
4. Ibid., 80.
5. Ibid.
6. Jill Bolte Taylor, *My Stroke of Insight* (Detroit, MI: Thorndike Press, 2006), large print edition, 29.
7. Lindblom, "Science," 82.
8. Ibid., 86.
9. Hans Jonas, *The Imperative of Responsibility: In Search of an Ethics for the Technological Age* (Chicago, IL: University of Chicago, 1985), 11.

10. Jamais Cascio, "It's Time to Cool the Planet," *Wall Street Journal*, 15 June 2009, pp. R1–R2.

11. Pope Pius XI, "Encyclical *Quadragesimo Anno* of Pius XI," 15 May 1931; available from www.vatican.va/holy_father/ pius_xi/encyclicals/documents/hf_p-xi_enc_19310515_ quadragesimo-anno_en.html, Internet, accessed 22 June 2009.

12. *Federalist Papers*, no. 56; http://avalon.law.yale.edu/18th_ century/fed56.asp;F; accessed 15 May 2009.

13. William A. Cohen, *A Class with Drucker: The Lost Lessons of the World's Great Management Teacher* (New York: AMA-COM, 2008), 59.

14. James Surowiecki, *The Wisdom of Crowds: Why the Many Are Smarter than the Few and How Collective Wisdom Shapes Business, Economics, Societies, and Nations* (New York: Random House, 2005), 79.

15. For other problems, see Cass R. Sunstein, "Introduction: Notes on Feminist Thought," *Ethics* 99, no. 2 (January, 1989): 219–228.

16. Hannah Arendt, "Crisis in Culture," in Arendt, *Between Past and Future: Six Exercises in Political Thought* (New York: Meridian, 1961), 220–221.

17. Ravi Shankar, http://www.ravishankar.org/indian_music. html; accessed 1 September 2008.

18. Matthew Crawford, "The Case for Working with Your Hands," *New York Times*, 24 May 2009; http:// www.nytimes.com/2009/05/24/magazine/24labor-t.html? scp=3&sq=matthew%20crawford&st=cse; accessed 25 May 2009.

19. Ibid.

20. Ibid.

21. Ibid.

22. Pat Kane, review of *The Craftsman*, by Richard Sennett, *The Scottish Review of Books* 4, no. 2 (2008); http://theplayethic. typepad.com/play_journal/2008/05/play-and-craft.html; accessed 3 July 2008.

23. Charles Handy, *The Age of Paradox* (Cambridge, MA: Harvard Business School Press, 1995), 142–143.

24. Shankar Basu and Roger G. Schroeder, "Incorporating Judgments in Sales Forecasts," *Interfaces* 7, no. 3 (1977): 18–25.

25. Rebecca Yarbrough, "Reducing Unintended Consequences: A Process for Planning," *Best Practices Forum*; http://www.cogsconnect.org/ccog/index.php?option=com_content&task=view&id=18&Itemid=52; accessed 9 October 2008.

26. Jan Richards, "Introduction to Universal Design," talk given at the Adaptive Technology Resource Centre, University of Toronto; http://anarch.ie.utoronto.ca/courses/mie240/UniversalDesign.ppt; accessed 7 September 2007.

27. Dietrich Dörner, *The Logic of Failure: Recognizing and Avoiding Error in Complex Situations* (New York: Basic Books, 1997), 16–17.

28. Ibid., 18.

29. Liz Moyer, "Bank of America: Why They Can't Boot Ken," *Forbes*, 30 April 2009; http://www.forbes.com/2009/04/30/bank-of-america-ken-lewis-business-wall-street-bofa.html; accessed 30 April 2009.

30. Joann S. Lublin and Cari Tuna, "Anticipating Corporate Crises: Boards Intensify Efforts to Review Risks and Dodge Disasters," *Wall Street Journal*, 22 September 2008; http://online.wsj.com/article/SB122202740338360765.html; accessed 22 September 2008.

31. Ibid.

32. Catherine Behan, "Sunstein: Court Not 'Moral Compass'," *The University of Chicago Chronicle* 17, no. 15 (30 April 1998); http://chronicle.uchicago.edu/980430/sunstein.shtml; accessed 1 January 2008.

33. Cass R. Sunstein, *One Case at a Time: Judicial Minimalism on the Supreme Court* (Cambridge, MA: Harvard University Press, 2001), passim.

34. Behan, "Sunstein."

35. Peter Eavis and David Reilly, "Losing Leverage: Some Firms Cut Debt in this Uncertain Era," *Wall Street Journal*, 7 April 2008, p. C1.

36. Ibid.

37. Both imported and American cars became more reliable, which likely was another factor in Americans' decision not to buy newer, more efficient cars.

38. Robert E. Grady, "Light Cars Are Dangerous Cars," *Wall Street Journal*, 22 May 2009; http://online.wsj.com/article/SB124294901851445311.html; accessed 23 May 2009.

39. Ibid.

40. Lisa Margonelli, "Don't Pay the Rich to Scrap Their Cars," *New York Times*, 16 May 2009; http://www.nytimes.com/2009/05/16/opinion/16margonelli.html; accessed 16 May 2009.

41. Mark Brenner, Stephanie Luce and Robert Pollin, "Intended versus Unintended Consequences: Evaluating the New Orleans Living Wage Ordinance," *Journal of Economic Issues* 36, no. 4 (2002): 843–875.

42. Richard H. Gifford and Harry Howe, "Regulation and Unintended Consequences: Thoughts on Sarbanes-Oxley," *CPA Journal* (June 2004); http://www.nysscpa.org/cpajournal/2004/604/perspectives/p6.htm; accessed 10 April 2007.

43. Sharla A. Stewart, "Can Behavioral Economics Save Us from Ourselves?" *University of Chicago Magazine* (February 2005): 37–42.

44. Ibid., 40.

45. Maureen A. Mahoney and Barbara Yngvesson, "The Construction of Subjectivity and the Paradox of Resistance: Reintegrating Feminist Anthropology and Psychology," *Signs* 18, no. 1 (Autumn, 1992): 46.

46. Wikipedia, "Simon-Ehrlich Wager;" http://en.wikipedia.org/wiki/Simon-Ehrlich_wager; accessed 19 February 2007.

47. Ed Regis, "The Doomslayer," *Wired* 5, no. 2 (February 1997); http://www.wired.com/wired/archive/5.02/ffsimon.html; accessed 29 February 2007.

48. Ibid.

49. David Hackett Fischer, *The Dream of Champlain* (New York: Simon & Schuster, 2008), 141–142, 530–531.

50. Ibid., 142.

51. Ibid., 530.

Conclusion

1. Nigel Dower, *World Ethics: The New Agenda* (Edinburgh: Edinburgh University Press, 1998), 166.

Bibliography

Akerlof, George A. and Robert J. Shiller. *Animal Spirits: How Human Psychology Drives the Economy and Why It Matters for Global Capitalism*. Princeton, NJ: Princeton University Press, 2009.

Arendt, Hannah. *Between Past and Future: Six Exercises in Political Thought*. New York: Meridian, 1961.

Aristotle. *Nicomachean Ethics*. Trans. W. D. Ross. Lawrence, KS: Digireads.com, 2005.

Basu, Shankar and Roger G. Schroeder. "Incorporating Judgments in Sales Forecasts." *Interfaces* 7, no. 3 (1977): 18–25.

Behan, Catherine. "Sunstein: Court Not 'Moral Compass'." *The University of Chicago Chronicle* 17, no. 13 (30 April 1998); http://chronicle.uchicago.edu/980430/sunstein.shtml; accessed 1 May 2007.

Berry, Christopher J. *Social Theory of the Scottish Enlightenment*. Edinburgh: Edinburgh University Press, 1997.

Botkin, James, Mahdi Elmandjra and Mircea Malita. *No Limits to*

Learning: Bridging the Human Gap. Oxford: Pergamon Press, 1979.

Boudon, Raymond. *The Art of Self-Persuasion.* Malden, MA: Blackwell Publishers Inc., 1994.

——. *The Logic of Social Action.* London: Routledge & Kegan Paul, 1981.

Brenner, Mark, Stephanie Luce and Robert Pollin. "Intended versus Unintended Consequences: Evaluating the New Orleans Living Wage Ordinance." *Journal of Economic Issues* 36, no. 4 (2002): 843–875.

Cascio, Jamais. "It's Time to Cool the Planet." *Wall Street Journal,* 15 June 2009: R1–R2.

Chugh, Dolly and Max H. Bazerman. "Bounded Awareness: What You Fail to See Can Hurt You." *Mind & Society* 6 (2007): 1–18.

Cohen, William A. *A Class with Drucker: The Lost Lessons of the World's Greatest Management Teacher.* New York: AMACOM, 2007.

Crawford, Matthew. "The Case for Working with Your Hands." *New York Times,* Sunday Magazine, 24 May 2009; http://www.nytimes.com/2009/05/24/magazine/24labor-t.html?scp =3&sq=matthew%20crawford&st=cse; accessed 25 May 2009.

Daum, Julie H. and Thomas J. Neff. "The Numbers Are In . . . and Soundly Rising." *Directors & Boards* (Fall, 2003): 23–24.

DeLeire, Thomas. "The Unintended Consequences of the Americans with Disabilities Act." *Regulation* 23, no. 1 (2000): 21–24.

Dörner, Dietrich. *The Logic of Failure: Recognizing and Avoiding Error in Complex Situations.* New York: Basic Books, 1997.

Dower, Nigel. *World Ethics: The New Agenda.* Edinburgh: Edinburgh University Press, 1998.

Elster, Jon. *Logic and Society, Contradictions and Possible Worlds.* London: Wiley, 1978.

Federalist Papers; http://avalon.law.yale.edu/18th_century/fed56.asp; accessed 15 May 2009.

Fox, Craig R. and Amos Tversky. "A Belief-Based Account of

Decision-Making under Uncertainty." *Management Science* 44, no. 7: 879–895.

Gifford, Richard H. and Harry Howe. "Regulation and Unintended Consequences: Thoughts on Sarbanes-Oxley." *CPA Journal* (June, 2004); http://www.nysscpa.org/cpajournal/2004/604/perspectives/p6.htm; accessed 15 November 2007.

Gilligan, Carol. *In a Different Voice*. Cambridge, MA: Harvard University Press, 1982.

Grieve, Andrew and Steve Dickinson. "China's New Labor Law"; http://www.chinalawblog.com/2008/05/chinas_new_labor_contract_law_1.html; accessed 10 April 2007.

Handy, Charles. *The Age of Paradox*. Cambridge, MA: Harvard Business School Press, 1994.

Harris, Jared D. and Philip Bromiley. "Incentives to Cheat: The Influence of Executive Compensation and Firm Performance on Financial Misrepresentation." *Organization Science* 18, no. 3 (2006): 350–367.

Herbert, George. *Jacula Prudentum*. London: T.M. for T. Garthwait, 1651.

Herodotus. *History*. Trans. A. D. Godley. Cambridge, MA: Harvard University Press, 1975.

Holtz, Robert L. "Testosterone May Fuel Stock-Market Success, Or Make Traders Tipsy." *Wall Street Journal*, 18 April 2008, B1.

Jian, Guowei. "Unpacking Unintended Consequences in Organizational Change: A Process Model." *Management Communication Quarterly* 21, no. 1 (2007): 5–28.

Johansson, Petter, Lars Hall and S. Sikstrom. "From Change Blindness to Choice Blindness." *Psychologia* 51, no. 2 (2008): 142–155.

Jonas, Hans. *The Imperative of Responsibility: In Search of an Ethics for the Technological Age*. Chicago, IL: University of Chicago Press, 1985.

——. *The Phenomenon of Life: Toward a Philosophical Biology*. Evanston, IL: Northwestern University Press, 2001.

Kane, Pat. Review of *The Craftsman*, by Richard Sennett. *The*

Scottish Review of Books 4, no. 2 (2008); http://theplayethic. typepad.com/play_journal/2008/05/play-and-craft.html; accessed 3 July 2008.

Kant, Immanuel. *Ground of the Metaphysics of Morals*. Trans. H. J. Paton. New York: Harper Perennial, 1964.

Kaplan, James A. "The Perverse Effect of Credit Default Swaps: A Catastrophe in the Making." Chairman's Corner, *Audit Integrity*, 17 June 2008; http://auditintegrity.com; accessed 17 June 2008.

Kennedy, Gavin. "Adam Smith's Invisible Hand: From Metaphor to Myth." Paper presented at the 34th Annual Meeting of the History of Economics Society, George Mason University, Fairfax, Virginia, 10 June 2007.

Kleyn, Tarina and Jürgens Jozefowicz. "Wasteland Created by Human Hands." *Hamburg Evening News*, 28–29 December 1985.

Koehn, Daryl. *Rethinking Feminist Ethics*. London: Routledge, 1998.

Kristie, James. "A Delicious Irony in Governance Ideology." *Directors & Boards* (Summer, 1999).

Laffer, Arthur and Stephen Moore. "Soak the Rich, Lose the Rich." *Wall Street Journal*, 18 May 2009; http://online.wsj. com/article/SB124260067214828295.html; accessed 18 May 2009.

Lee, Danielle. "Mattel Recalls More China-Manufactured Toys." *CRO Newsletter*, 5 September 2007; http://www.thecro.com/ node/521; accessed 1 October 2007.

Lindblom, Charles E. "The Science of 'Muddling Through'." *Public Administration Review* 19 (Spring, 1959): 79–88.

Locke, John. *An Essay Concerning Human Understanding*; http:// arts.cuhk.edu.hk/Philosophy/Locke/echu/ed; accessed 13 June 2008.

Lueck, Dean and Jeffrey Michael. "Preemptive Habitat Destruction under the Endangered Species Act." *The Journal of Law and Economics* 46 (2003): 27–60.

Mahoney, Maureen A. and Barbara Yngvesson. "The Construction of Subjectivity and the Paradox of Resistance: Reintegrating

Feminist Anthropology and Psychology." *Signs* 18, no. 1 (Autumn, 1992): 44–73.

McKinley, William and Andreas G. Scherer. "Some Unanticipated Consequences of Organizational Restructuring." *Academy of Management Review* 25 (2000): 735–753.

Merton, Robert K. *On Social Structure and Science*. Chicago, IL: University of Chicago Press, 1996.

——. "The Unintended Consequences of Purposive Social Action." *American Sociological Review* 1, no. 6 (December, 1936): 894–904.

Mill, John Stuart. *Utilitarianism*. New York: Dover Publications, 2007.

Mises, Ludwig von. *Human Action: A Treatise on Economics*. Indianapolis, IN: Liberty Fund, 2007.

Pope Pius XI. "Encyclical *Quadragesimo Anno* of Pius XI." 15 May 1931; http://www.vatican.va/holy_father/pius_xi/encyclicals/documents/hf_p-xi_enc_19310515_quadragesimo-anno_en.html; accessed 22 June 2009.

Rahe, Paul A. *Soft Despotism*. New Haven, CT: Yale University Press, 2009.

Regis, Ed. "The Doomslayer." *Wired* 5, no. 2 (February 1997); http://www.wired.com/wired/archive/5.02/ffsimon.html; accessed 29 February 2007.

Richards, Jan. "Introduction to Universal Design." Unpublished paper. Adaptive Technology Resource Centre, University of Toronto, 2007.

Senge, Peter. *The Fifth Discipline: The Art and Practice of the Learning Organization*. New York: Random House Business Books, 1993.

Sharkey, Catherine M. "Unintended Consequences of Medical Malpractice Damages Caps." *NYU Law Review* 80 (2005): 391–512.

Simons, D. J. and C. F. Chabris. "Gorillas in Our Midst: Sustained Inattentional Blindness for Dynamic Events." *Perception* 28, no. 9 (1999): 1059–1074.

Smith, Zadie. "E. M. Forster, Middle Manager: The BBC Talks of E. M. Forster, 1929–1969." *New York Review of Books* 55,

no. 13 (14 August 2008); http://www.nybooks.com/articles/
21692; accessed 5 December 2008.

Stewart, Sharla A. "Can Behavioral Economics Save Us from
Ourselves?" *University of Chicago Magazine* (February, 2005):
37–42.

Sunstein, Cass R. "Introduction: Notes on Feminist Thought."
Ethics 99, no. 2 (January, 1989): 219–228.

———. *One Case at a Time: Judicial Minimalism on the Supreme
Court.* Cambridge, MA: Harvard University Press, 2001.

Surowiecki, James. *The Wisdom of Crowds: Why the Many Are
Smarter than the Few and How Collective Wisdom Shapes
Business, Economics, Societies, and Nations.* New York: Anchor,
2005.

Taylor, Jill Bolte. *My Stroke of Insight.* Detroit, MI: Thorndike
Press, 2006. Large print edition.

Tolkien, J. R. R. *The Hobbit.* Boston, MA: Houghton Mifflin
Company, 1994.

Ulanowicz, Robert E. "Life after Newton: An Ecological Metaphysic." *BioSystems* 50, no. 2 (1999): 127–142.

Vera-Munoz, Sandra C. "Corporate Governance Reforms:
Redefined Expectations of Audit Committee Responsi-
bilities and Effectiveness." *Journal of Business Ethics* 62, no. 2
(December, 2005): 115–127.

Wodatch, John. "ADA Audio Conference," 18 May 2004; http://
www.ada-audio.org/Archives/?type=transcript&id=2004-
05–18; accessed 8 February 2008.

Wolin, Richard. *Heidegger's Children: Hannah Arendt, Karl Lowith,
Hans Jonas, and Herbert Marcuse.* Princeton, NJ: Princeton
University Press, 2001.

Yack, Bernard. "Injustice and the Victim's Voice." *Michigan Law
Review* 89 (1991): 1334–1343.

Yarbrough, Rebecca. "Reducing Unintended Consequences: A
Process for Planning." *Best Practices Forum*; http://
www.cogsconnect.org/ccog/index.php?option=com_content
&task=view&id=18&Itemid=52; accessed 9 October 2008.

Zhang, Daowei. "Endangered Species and Timber Harvesting:
The Case of Red-Cockaded Woodpeckers." *Economic
Inquiry* 42, no. 1 (2004): 150–165.

Index